A RIVER AGAIN

Secretary West Chester Fish & Game

A RIVER AGAIN

The Story of the Schuylkill River Project

Chari Towne 1/16/15

CHARI TOWNE

Delaware Riverkeeper Network Press

Printed in the United States of America
Published 2012.
First Edition

For information about permission to reproduce selections from this book, contact the Delaware Riverkeeper Network, 925 Canal Street, Suite 3701, Bristol, PA 19007.

Delaware Riverkeeper Network Press is a project of the Delaware Riverkeeper Network. For more information, go to http://www.delawareriverkeeper.org/.

Designed by C. Towne

ISBN-10: 0-985987200 (hard cover)
ISBN-13: 987-0-9859872-0-6 (hard cover)

This book was prepared to provide information on the Schuylkill River Project. References are provided for informational purposes only and do not constitute endorsement of any websites or other sources. Readers should be aware that the websites listed in this book may change.

This project was funded in part by the Pennsylvania Department of Conservation and Natural Resources through the Schuylkill River Heritage Area grant program.

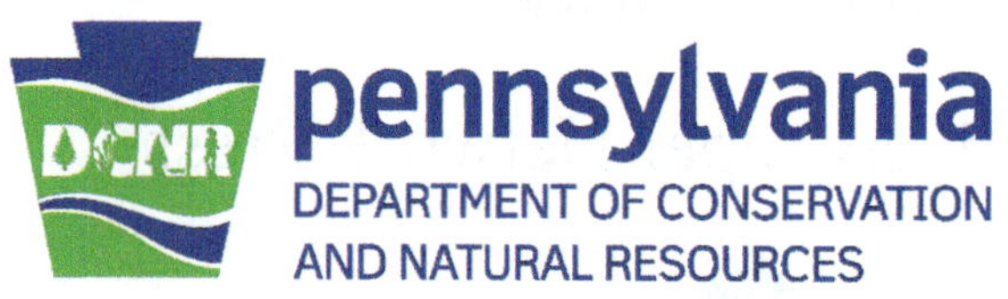

Dedication

I came to the Schuylkill years ago with no knowledge of its past. I got to know the river from a rowing shell, up close and very personally. Because of my time spent training on the river, and the memories associated with rowing there, the Schuylkill will always hold a special place in my life. Every day I wish I was in a boat on the water.

Because these were not my native waters, there was much to learn about the watershed that feeds the Schuylkill as well as Pennsylvania. Over my years here, I have learned a great deal from leaders in environmental protection as well as common men and women. Sadly, some of these good people are not here to see this book come to be: Richard James, Carl Dusinberre, Dick Albert, Eleanor Morris, and Bob Smith.

But I continue to learn every day from those who are working now to make the waters of Pennsylvania and their local streams clean and healthier: John Johnson and Pete Goodman, Alice Lang, Bill Reichert and Robert Hughes, and Michael Hendricks to name a few.

This book is dedicated to colleagues, past and present, and all people working to leave a legacy of clean streams for future generations.

Contents

Preface

Acknowledgements

Introduction

Bad Reputation	**5**
The Country's Dirtiest River	**11**
Stone Coal	**17**
A Trifling Inconvenience	**27**
James Henderson Duff	**41**
An Actionable Wrong	**49**
The Worst First	**57**
Working on the Project	**75**
Selling Silt	**89**
Canaries of the Stream	**125**
The River Endures	**137**
Acid to Reading	**153**
Breaking with the Past	**163**

Notes

Preface

I would like to say that preparing a history of the Schuylkill River cleanup was done by choice, but that would be wrong. It would be more accurate to say that the Schuylkill River Project found me. My first encounter with the project came about shortly after I joined the staff of the Delaware Riverkeeper Network 17 years ago with the donation of a rare and fragile copy of the *Final Report of the Schuylkill River Project Engineers.* At the time, the inscription in the book—"To Bill Moll, in appreciation for his help in this great Project, E. McCawley"—didn't mean anything to me. Bill Moll and E. McCawley were just names. I would later learn that both served in the Pennsylvania Department of Forests and Waters during the Schuylkill River Project, E. McCawley (Commander Edmund S. McCawley) as Deputy Secretary and Bill Moll (Wilford P. Moll) as District Forester.

A few years later, Richard L. Rosendale walked into our field office with a roll of maps and a box of papers, records from his time with the Schuylkill River Project that he had kept with him for over 50 years. Rosendale had kept the records thinking that someday he would use them to write a book about the cleanup. But he and his wife were down-sizing to a smaller home, and he would no longer have room for them. Rosendale donated his papers to us and they joined the *Final Report of the Schuylkill River Project Engineers* on a shelf in our offices, but a seed had been planted. The full story of the Schuylkill River Project deserves wider recognition; it is time that story is told.

Most recently, the Delaware Riverkeeper Network was able to assist in the preservation of documents relating to the Schuylkill River Project. When the Pennsylvania Department of Environmental Protection, which had inherited the files, needed to dispose of the documents to make room in a Kernsville warehouse, the Delaware Riverkeeper Network accepted ownership of the files and, with the assistance of Union Township in Berks County, we held the files until the Montgomery County Community College could accept them into its Archives and Special Collections. These documents are being processed and will become part of the College's Schuylkill River Archival Collection where students, researchers, and private citizens wanting to better understand the river's past can access them.

Once you learn about the Schuylkill River Project, you can see its impacts on the landscape yet today, but few remain with us now to share their memories of this remarkable cleanup. Fewer still remain who can say they were among those who helped clean up what was once considered this country's dirtiest river.

In my position with an environmental organization working to protect and defend the Delaware River and its tributaries—including the Schuylkill River, it is my privilege to be able to highlight this important project and to share the lessons it holds for current environmental restoration work. The Schuylkill River Project was a large scale undertaking encompassing over 100 miles of river. Undertaken from 1947 to 1951, it was the first environmental cleanup carried out by a government agency, and it is among the earliest river restoration efforts in this country, predating other river restoration efforts by decades.

Habitat restoration has been one of the Delaware Riverkeeper Network's programs since 1992. The Delaware Riverkeeper Network advocates for water quality and habitat protection; helps organize local communities to protect local streams; monitors the health of the Delaware and its tributaries; provides technical expertise that addresses complex watershed issues; and undertakes legal action when necessary to enforce environmental laws.

Since the establishment of its habitat restoration program, the Delaware Riverkeeper Network has helped install over 100 projects throughout the watershed. From its earliest work on the Cooper and Schuylkill Rivers, the Delaware Riverkeeper Network has strived to implement innovative, cost-efficient, and ecologically sound restoration projects. The Schuylkill River Project offers lessons for our habitat restoration work, but the project's connections extend across all the Delaware Riverkeeper Network's programs.

For that matter, the Schuylkill River Project offers lessons for those working in the environmental field, outdoor enthusiasts, history buffs, Pennsylvanians of every stripe, even politicians. And for anyone who has spent a day on the Schuylkill or along its banks, the river has been waiting to share its story. I hope you enjoy reading it.

Chari Towne
Schuylkill Watershed Specialist
Delaware Riverkeeper Network

Acknowledgements

I would first like to thank Delaware Riverkeeper Maya van Rossum and the Delaware Riverkeeper Network for entertaining the idea of this book and sparing the time to make it possible.

This book would not exist without the financial support provided by the Pennsylvania Department of Conservation and Natural Resources through the Schuylkill River Heritage Area Grant Program, The William Penn Foundation and The Jerlyn Foundation. I am deeply gratified that these organizations saw value in this project. I am also grateful for the trust bestowed on me by Tim Fenchel and Kurt Zwikl, Andrew Johnson, and Carolyn Holleran on behalf of these funders.

The Schuylkill River Project and the people who were a part of it were brought to life for me by Richard L. Rosendale, Daniel E. and Nancy Ludwig, Robert Williams, John Cairns, Jr., Darla Donald, Thomas Dolan, IV, Robert Phillips, Pat and Robert Adams, George Heckman and Chet Epting. They shared freely their time and memories with me. I am in their debt.

I also want to thank Michael C. Korb and Michael J. Allwein, Department of Environmental Protection; Steve Cotler, Stoudt's Ferry Preparation Company; Roger Thomas, Megan Gibes, and Daniel Thomas, Academy of Natural Sciences of Drexel University, Todd Moses, Skelly and Loy, Inc.; William C. Brunner and Joe Forrest, Spring Ford Area Historical Society; Laura Catalano, Schuylkill River Heritage Area; Faith Zerbe, Elizabeth Koniers Brown, Doris Brooke, and intern Daniel P. Murray, Delaware Riverkeeper Network; John Salaneck, III, Union Township; Russ Braun, Jones Township; Susan Hughes, Pennsylvania Federation of Sportsmen's Clubs; Gregg Adams; Donald Kucharik; John Mikowychok; Christian Devol; and Ted Danforth. Their contributions enriched this work.

The research for this book was assisted by Lawrence Greene, Archives and Special Collections of the Montgomery County Community College; Greg Soule, Pennsylvania Senate Library; Heidi Mays, Pennsylvania House of Representatives; David Osgood,

Albright College; Adam Levine, Philadelphia Water Department; and the staffs of the Pennsylvania State Archives, the Chester County Library Inter-Library Loan Department, the Special Collections of West Chester University, the *Pennsylvania Game News, and* the *Pennsylvania Angler.*

The Delaware Riverkeeper Network's Mary Ellen Noble acted as copy editor. I greatly appreciated her persistence, tact and enthusiasm for a good story and her efforts to help make this a better one. My thanks also go to proofreaders M. Irvil Kear, Ian Palmer, Sue Young, Lauren Imgrund, and Laurie Rosenberg for their attention to detail and suggested revisions. Any errors are mine.

Grateful thanks go to my friends and family for their understanding during the writing of this book. And finally to my most patient husband, Jay Gregg, my special thanks for his encouragement, for being a sounding board, for his editing, and for appreciating how much this project meant to me.

Thank you all.

Introduction

When Chari Towne first approached me about having the Schuylkill River National & State Heritage Area provide a grant to assist with the publishing of a book on the history of the cleanup of the Schuylkill River, it didn't take me very long to say, "Please apply." The University of Wisconsin grad, Olympic rower, and Schuylkill Watershed Specialist for the Delaware Riverkeeper Network was on to something that has been neglected for far too long.

The Schuylkill River Heritage Area was created by an Act of Congress in 2000 because of the role the Schuylkill River Valley played in the American, Industrial, and Environmental Revolutions. To the average person the first two revolutions are quite obvious. George Washington's army fought to prevent the capture of Philadelphia by the British in 1777 during the American Revolution. Later the discovery of coal and the construction of the Schuylkill Canal and then the railroads heralded the movement of coal from Schuylkill County to Philadelphia, igniting the Industrial Revolution. But the Environmental Revolution? What could possibly have taken place here that would warrant that title? Over a hundred years of industrial and mining activities in the region imperiled the Schuylkill River Valley's water resources. This led to environmental reclamation and water quality restoration on a massive scale.

In 2003, when I first became the executive director of the Schuylkill River Greenway Association, which manages the Schuylkill River Heritage Area, I wanted to learn how the region dealt with this environmental reclamation of the river. But the only resources that existed were some unrecorded oral histories and a few faded newspaper clippings. Our organization at that time didn't even have a copy of the government report entitled, *Final Report of the Schuylkill River Project Engineers*, dated July 1, 1951. This document was only available in a limited quantity and in a three-ring binder. Unless you worked in the desilting operation or lived along the river since the 1940s, chances are you had little understanding of what occurred between 1947 and 1951. Nevertheless, the Schuylkill River

Project was an extraordinary undertaking representing the first large scale environmental cleanup ever performed by a government agency in the United States. Now that was revolutionary!

The Schuylkill River Heritage Area's management plan has as one of its goals to "support educational and research initiatives that teach the public about the Schuylkill River Valley's historical, cultural and national heritage." With Ms. Towne's proposal, we now had an opportunity to support and promote the telling of this story and to fulfill this goal.

A River Again, The Story of the Schuylkill River Project, is a narrative of business, economic development, politics, and the environment and how, after decades of abuse and neglect, the will to clean up the Schuylkill River was eventually found.

It is an historian's dream to write about a topic that has never been written about before, a chapter of our history that few people know about. Chari Towne has done just that, and her work will take its place alongside that of others who have recorded the history of the Schuylkill River region.

For this, the Schuylkill River Heritage Area and all of those who support our work, offer congratulations and thank her for adding to the historical literature of the Schuylkill River Valley.

Kurt D. Zwikl
Executive Director
Schuylkill River Heritage Area
June 2012

A RIVER AGAIN

The Story of the Schuylkill River Project

The Schuylkill River today is an example of what occurs when one looks only to the present and the future is disregarded.

— Department of Forests and Waters
Secretary Milo F. Draemel, 1948[1]

Bad Reputation

Take a walk along the Schuylkill River. On a bright sunny day, the river's surface reflects sunlight as a scattering of diamonds. The water is enticing. You want to be out on the Schuylkill, enjoying the river. Whether you are strolling along the Schuylkill in Philadelphia, Pottstown, or Reading, you will likely see someone who couldn't resist the call of the river. In Philadelphia, crews are out rowing on the three-mile long pool created by Fairmount Dam. In Mont Clare, anglers are fishing along the banks of the river or along the canal. At Kelly's Lock, north of Reading, kayakers are running rapids.

But too often, if you ask someone about the Schuylkill (pronounced SKOO - kil), you will hear that the river is polluted. The Schuylkill is dirty...an open sewer...a garbage dump. It's contaminated with toxic chemicals. The fish that swim in its waters are unsafe to eat. You boat on the Schuylkill at your own risk.

The Schuylkill River has a bad reputation. Stories about the polluted Schuylkill are passed along eagerly by those who don't have direct experience of the river. The more polluted, the better the story. The truth about the health of the river and what it means to the communities through which it flows is more complicated.

Today, the Schuylkill River and its tributaries provide drinking water for 1.5 million people[2]—in other words 12 of every 100 Pennsylvanians[3]—rely upon the Schuylkill River for drinking water. And water use in the Schuylkill River valley, at close to 200 gallons per capita per day (gcpd), is well above average.[4] Average per capita water use[5] in the Delaware River basin is just 133 gcpd.[6] The value of that untreated drinking water has been placed at $263,000 per day or $95,955,000 per year. The treated value of the water was estimated to be $483,856,000 per year.[7]

The Schuylkill's fishery includes native and introduced species—striped bass, American and gizzard shad, smallmouth bass, white sucker, catfish, sunfish and trout—and contributes millions to local economies. The total economic impact of fishing, including direct expenditures and induced and indirect income, was estimated at $43 million for Berks County alone.[8]

A River Again

In the late 1990s, the Pennsylvania Fish and Boat Commission began in earnest an effort to restore the migratory American shad to the Schuylkill River, setting as a goal 300,000 to 850,000 returning shad, a population the Pennsylvania Fish and Boat Commission believes could support 60,000 to 170,000 angler trips annually.[9] Since 1999, more than six million shad fry have been stocked in the river (M. Hendricks, personal communication, 2 May 2012). With an estimate of $50 to $75 spent per angler trip,[10] the income generated from a restored shad fishery could range from $3 million to $12.75 million each year.

Efforts to improve and install fish passage on the remaining dams on the river are paying off. In 2011, Pennsylvania Fish and Boat Commission biologists encountered an American shad below Black Rock Dam near Phoenixville. This sighting marked the first time the fish has been confirmed this far upstream—37 miles from the confluence with the Delaware River—since 1820.[11]

The Schuylkill River is also central to water-based recreation in the region. Well-known for its iconic images of rowing and Boathouse Row, the river is home to the Schuylkill Navy, the oldest amateur athletic governing body in the United States. The Schuylkill Navy is made up of the 10 clubs on Boathouse Row as well as high school and college rowing programs. From April to November, the Schuylkill is host to more than 20 regattas, not counting dual competitions among local college crews.[12] Among these regattas is the Dad Vail, the largest collegiate rowing event in the nation with over 100 rowing programs competing and up to 10,000 spectators. The economic impact of the Dad Vail Regatta for the City of Philadelphia has been estimated at $16 million.[13] Other regattas include the Independence Day Regatta, the largest summer club regatta in this country, and the Stotesbury Cup, the largest high school regatta in the world.

The Schuylkill in Philadelphia is home to several teams that compete in the fast growing sport of dragon boat racing, and the river is host to the annual Independence Dragon Boat Regatta and Philadelphia International Dragon Boat Festival. When Philadelphia hosted the World Dragon Boat Championships in 2001, the economic impact was estimated as high as $70 million.[14]

Paddle sports aren't limited to the lower Schuylkill in Philadelphia. The annual Schuylkill Sojourn gives interested paddlers the opportunity to paddle all or parts of the river for 112 miles from Schuylkill Haven to Philadelphia. Daily participation is limited to 100 people to ensure safety, and the weekend days regularly sell out weeks in advance. (K. Zwikl, personal communication, 23 March 2012).

Much of the Schuylkill is flat water presenting paddling opportunities for paddlers of all levels; however, Kelly's Lock above Reading offers more challenging whitewater and is a popular practice spot for advanced paddlers. With nearly 60 miles of the river within the borders of Berks County and paddling opportunities on the river's Tulpehocken and Maiden Creek tributaries, it's no surprise that canoeing and kayaking are estimated to contribute $31 million to Berks County's economy annually.[15]

Even when we can resist the river itself, we are still attracted to the open spaces and trails along its banks. The City of Philadelphia initially began acquiring land along the Schuylkill's banks in 1855 to protect its drinking water supply.[16] Those lands are now part of Fairmount Park which, at 9,200 acres, is one of the largest urban parks in the country. Much beloved by all Philadelphians, Fairmount Park provides drinking water protection, as well as an enhanced opportunity for events, public recreation, and environmental education.[17] And recent enhancements to Fairmount Park land along the Schuylkill are now providing City residents with recreational opportunities where train tracks once blocked river access. At Schuylkill Banks, a narrow strip of land eight miles long on the east bank of the tidal river, people can enjoy paddling, biking, walking, festivals, even fireworks on the Fourth of July.[18]

Upstream of Philadelphia in Pottstown, Riverfront Park is seeing an increase in park users as access to and recreational opportunities on both the Schuylkill River and the Schuylkill River Trail are made available. Counts of trail users conducted from May 2007 to October 2008 found over 65,000 people using that portion of the trail with usage jumping 27% during peak summer months from 2007 to 2008.[19]

The Schuylkill River also has a central role in the vision put forward recently in an economic development plan for the middle Schuylkill—the region from Valley Forge to Reading. The plan proposes economic development that is sustainable and compatible with the "hallmark cultural, recreational, and natural heritage destination" that the middle Schuylkill encompasses. The plan also includes as an objective protection of these hallmark resources.[20] Revitalization of towns with historic ties to the river—Phoenixville, Pottstown, Birdsboro, and Reading—is also an objective. River towns look to the Schuylkill for new opportunities. Planning efforts—like the proposal for the Lower Schuylkill to expand river access and the Schuylkill River Trail, improve stormwater management, and implement wetlands mitigation—reveal that the river is viewed as an asset, providing benefits and opportunities that are essential components of successful redevelopment.[21]

Clearly, the Schuylkill River is a vital amenity to the communities through which it flows. It provides drinking water, recreational opportunities, and aesthetic benefits; it supports local economies and is a defining force in the health of the region's ecology. It would seem the river has been given a bad rap. Still, as with many reputations, there is some truth at the heart of the Schuylkill's lingering bad reputation.

Not so long ago the Schuylkill was considered this country's dirtiest river. But there is more to the story than the cleanup of a polluted river. Other rivers once regarded as polluted are now also driving revitalization of communities. The Schuylkill's story is important not only because the river fell so far, but also because its cleanup came before all others. The concept of restoring a river was born on the Schuylkill River. The pollution of the Schuylkill was among the worst in the county, and its redemption offers lessons for how we interact with our rivers today.

The story of the Schuylkill cleanup is not well known, but it is one well worth telling.

In favor of the Schuylkill: The principal circumstance is the uncommon purity of its water.

— Benjamin Latrobe, 1799[22]

The Country's Dirtiest River

In 1799, a watering committee was established in Philadelphia and, swayed by Benjamin Latrobe's argument in its favor,[23] the committee chose the Schuylkill to supply the residents of Philadelphia with drinking water. A precursor to the Philadelphia Water Department, Philadelphia's watering committee became the first effort to supply an entire city with drinking water.[24] The Fairmount Water Works, built to provide that drinking water, became an international tourist attraction for both its architecture and engineering.[25]

The phrase "uncommon purity," which Benjamin Latrobe once used to describe the Schuylkill, is not likely to be applied today. In 1799, the river had not yet been affected by the Industrial Revolution. But the very water supply that the Schuylkill provided helped establish Philadelphia as a leader in manufacturing and would contribute to its pollution. Dr. Charles Cresson, chemist for the Philadelphia Board of Health for 15 years from 1864 to 1879, had studied the Schuylkill and understood how the properties of the river's waters made it attractive for industry:

> As a natural source for city supply, the river Schuylkill is unequalled. It furnishes a soft water containing but little mineral matter, running in a shallow stream over a rough rocky bed, with numerous rapids and cascades, which give it every opportunity for aeration and the destruction of organic matter. The limited amount of salts of lime and magnesia renders it a suitable and an economical water, not only for household use but also for most manufacturing purposes.[26]

But the Schuylkill of Cresson's day was much changed from the river that Latrobe had known. The Schuylkill River Navigation Company had been granted a charter in 1815 to make the Schuylkill navigable. From headwaters to mouth, the Schuylkill falls roughly 1,200 feet in just 130 miles. Although much of that fall is seen on the upper reaches, the gradient, current velocity, and a number of waterfalls along its length limited commerce. A navigable Schuylkill would mean that coal could more easily be moved to market from the headwaters.

In 1815, the blockade of the Port of Philadelphia during the War of 1812 was still fresh in memory. The disruption of coal imports spurred interest in the anthracite found in the Schuylkill's headwaters. Anthracite did not burn readily, which had limited interest in its use, but a rolling mill owner named Josiah White had discovered a method for burning anthracite.[27] Not surprisingly, White was among the initial partners of the Schuylkill Navigation Company.

To make the river navigable, Schuylkill Navigation created a slack water system, completed in 1824, that consisted of river pools behind 32 dams. The pools were linked by 72 sections of canal.

With a reliable public water supply, the Schuylkill canal for transportation, and anthracite for fuel, the stage was set for the Industrial Revolution in Philadelphia.

Cresson's studies of the Schuylkill, which also included causes of degradation, provide us with a picture of the kind of industry that had developed along the banks of the river by 1875:

> Refuse from bleaching and printing.
> " " scouring and dyeing.
> " " paper works (alkaline).
> " " gas works, tar, ammoniacal liquor, and wash from foul lime.[28]

But neither the discharges from these industries nor the sewage waste discharged to the river by Norristown concerned Cresson as much as the discharges from the cesspools and slaughterhouses which he notes were discharged directly into the pool created by Fairmount Dam, the pool from which the City drew its water supply. Cresson was concerned that the cesspools and slaughterhouses contributed to outbreaks of yellow fever, cholera, and typhoid. Despite his concern, however, Cresson did not recommend banning the discharge of the slaughterhouse waste to the river; he simply suggested it be diverted by channels to discharge below Fairmount Dam.

Interestingly, Cresson believed that a few drops of sulfuric acid in drinking water provided some protection from these diseases. And there again, he believed the Schuylkill had advantages:

> In addition to the natural advantages possessed by the river Schuylkill for the purification of the water, it happens that it receives from many sources quite large amounts of free sulfuric acid. ...This acid is derived chiefly from the decomposition of the pyrites of the coal waste at the mines near its source and from the refuse of the iron furnaces erected along the course of the river.[29]

Still Cresson seemed to have reservations about the river as the City's drinking water supply: "The pollution of the Schuylkill River has been increased to such an extent as occasionally to class the water as 'unwholesome.' "[30]

The idea of protecting Philadelphia's water supply by preserving open space along the Schuylkill dates back to at least the 1840s when city residents urged the acquisition of land along the river. The first such acquisition in 1844 was the estate known as Lemon Hill which had once belonged to Robert Morris, a signer of the Declaration of Independence who has been called the financier of the American Revolution. In addition to support from city residents, the purchase of Lemon Hill was recommended by the College of Physicians of Philadelphia to protect the City's water supply.[31] Lemon Hill was the first acquisition of land that would eventually become Fairmount Park.

After 1855, the City of Philadelphia would acquire additional lands along the Schuylkill to protect the drinking water supply, but as the region's population grew and industry expanded, the problems only seemed to get worse. On July 10th, 1882, the *New York Times* reported that for a distance of sixty miles, the Schuylkill was dark green in color and appeared soapy. Fish of all species were dying by the thousands.[32] By 1885, engineers at the Philadelphia Water Department had determined that deforestation in the river's headwaters had "deprived the river of that power of conservation which is given by woodland" and depleted river flows during dry periods.[33] On April 16th, 1891, an outbreak of typhoid in Philadelphia was reported with the greatest mortality "found in four wards that use water supplied directly from the dirty Schuylkill."[34] On November 2nd, 1892, the *New York Times* reported on the Schuylkill burning when a thin scum of oil on the river near Point Breeze was accidentally set on fire.[35]

By 1885, the river had become so polluted that a consensus had emerged: ultimately, the City would have to abandon the Schuylkill as its water supply. From mine drainage and coal silt in the headwaters to sewage discharges in the middle Schuylkill to the industrial region around Philadelphia, into the Schuylkill were poured "all the waste matters of a large and busy population."[36] In less than one hundred years the Schuylkill had been transformed from "waters of uncommon purity" to "objectionable."[37] "No fish can exist in it, nor can human beings drink it."[38] Attention began to turn away from the Schuylkill as the source of Philadelphia's drinking water and back to the Delaware River.

Unfortunately for the City of Philadelphia, which remained committed to the Schuylkill for a significant portion of its water supply, the river's problems were only going to get worse as a new century dawned.

Contamination of the streams in the coal region has been in progress for more than fifty years.

— Pennsylvania Water Supply Commission, 1916[39]

Stone Coal

Roughly 130 miles northwest of Philadelphia rise the Schuylkill River's headwaters, near Tuscarora, Pennsylvania. Schuylkill County, where the river begins, was named for the river. Should you travel to the Schuylkill's headwaters, you will find yourself in the southern coalfields of Pennsylvania's anthracite region, among the richest deposits of coal in the world. Although anthracite was known to exist in Pennsylvania as early as 1698,[40] its discovery in the Schuylkill's headwaters came later, after 1760.

Initially, there was little demand for anthracite, because it was difficult to burn. Several years passed before anthracite was regarded as a usable fuel source. The merits of anthracite as fuel were still not apparent to manufacturing interests in Philadelphia in 1800 when William Morris arrived with a wagonload of anthracite from Pottsville. Though Morris was unable to sell his anthracite, hard coal was soon to become a major fuel source for our nation's growth.

In 1808, Jesse Fell, a Wilkes-Barre tavern owner and political leader, made a breakthrough. Fell developed a method of burning anthracite on an iron grate. With an adequate supply of air, the coal burned successfully. Mines were opened in the Schuylkill's headwaters by 1814. In 1820, 365 tons of coal transported to Philadelphia was recorded as the first regular shipment of anthracite to market. But these first shipments of coal came to Philadelphia by wagon or via the Lehigh and Delaware Rivers. Although small amounts of coal were transported on the Schuylkill around this time, Philadelphia would have to wait until 1824 and the completion of the Schuylkill Navigation system before coal in any quantity would arrive via the Schuylkill.

Anthracite became the fuel of the Industrial Revolution and fed an energy-hungry nation during two world wars. By 1913, 80 million tons of coal were being extracted from the anthracite fields annually. In 1917, coal production reached a peak with over 100 million tons extracted. Coal production has steadily declined since this high point. Pennsylvania's current anthracite production is approximately 1.8 million tons annually.

To understand the properties of anthracite, you need go back in time 400 million years. Warm and humid conditions encouraged the growth of lush forests with mosses, lichens, jungle vines, tropical seed ferns, and non-flowering trees. Vast amounts of plant material thrived, died, and underwent slow decomposition. Biological and chemical processes converted these decaying organisms into peat, a spongy brown material.

Over long periods of time, layers of peat were compacted together by physical and chemical processes. Continued pressure converted the compressed peat to lignite, a low-grade coal. As the forces of pressure and time continued, lignite was transformed into bituminous or soft coal. Subsequently, the folding and faulting that formed the mountains of Schuylkill County produced friction and heat that further transformed the soft coal. These mountain-forming processes expelled oxygen and hydrogen which increased the carbon content and created anthracite, the highest grade of coal. Also known as stone coal or hard coal, anthracite is a high carbon, low sulfur fuel with high BTU values.

Anthracite is among the most valuable of coals, but distribution of reserves is very limited. Pennsylvania's hard coal region spans an eleven-county area that encompasses over 3,000 square miles; however, only a small portion of this area, about 484 square miles, is underlain with workable anthracite coal seams. Most of Pennsylvania's anthracite is concentrated in Carbon, Lackawanna, Luzerne, Northumberland, and Schuylkill Counties. A semi-anthracite coal is also found in Sullivan County.

Pennsylvania's anthracite deposits are divided into four distinct fields: the northern, western middle, eastern middle, and southern. It has been estimated that these four fields constitute 5% of the world's anthracite and 95% of the northern hemisphere's anthracite.

Pennsylvania's pre-mining reserves of anthracite and semi-anthracite have been estimated at 23 billion tons.[41] As much as 12 billion tons of anthracite reserves may yet remain. The U.S. Energy Information Administration puts Pennsylvania's anthracite reserve base—those reserves with the potential to be recovered given technology and economic conditions in the foreseeable future—at 7.188 billion tons with just 759 million tons considered currently recoverable without regard to cost.[42]

Portions of the southern anthracite field underlie the Schuylkill River's headwaters. This coal field runs for roughly 55 miles from Halifax to Nesquehoning and, at 181 square miles, is the largest of the four fields. The southern field is surrounded by mountain ridges and contains coal beds with the steepest pitches of all the anthracite fields.

Anthracite is popular for home heating because it burns slowly while emitting little smoke. Today, the main markets for anthracite are power generation, residential and commercial heating; as carbon for industry and manufacturing; and as a medium for water filtration. In the U.S. in 2012, roughly 44% of electricity is still generated from coal, and projections through 2035 have coal retaining the largest share of U.S. electricity generation.[43] The price of coal has been rising, after declines from 1990 to 2000. Mining companies are reporting growing demand for anthracite[44] with an average sale price of $166.30 per ton in the first quarter of 2012 compared with a price of $134.25 during the same period in 2011.[45]

Before raw coal can be burned, it must be cleaned and processed. Cleaning, or preparation, involves removal of the slate or other rock material and other impurities that are extracted along with the coal. Large chunks of coal must be broken down into marketable sizes. Coal is also sized for end use. For example, stove- (2-7/16″ to 1-5/8″) and chestnut- (7/8″ to 1-1/2″) sized anthracite are used in hand-fired stoves. Buckwheat (9/16″ x 5/16″) and rice (5/16″ x 3/16″) are used with stoves with automatic feeding or "stoker" systems.

No effort was made to prepare the first coal that was mined in the Schuylkill's headwaters. The raw, or run-of-mine, coal was sent to market as it was, but soon the removal of rock and other materials and sizing of coal became standard practice.[46]

Smaller sizes of coal were harder to burn, but the adoption of stoker systems increased demand for them; however, the removal of impurities from smaller sizes of coal was difficult. Until the 1900s, much of the coal sized 7/8" and smaller was considered a waste product.[47] These coal fines, or culm, along with rock material and other debris that had been removed from the raw coal, were simply dumped into piles. Over time, these culm banks grew into black mountains towering over mine operations and the adjacent patch towns. Culm banks can have hazardous, unstable slopes. They can catch fire and burn. Coal fines can wash from the culm banks into streams. When rainwater infiltrates into these culm banks, the acid that forms pollutes streams. And because culm piles pre-date federal regulation, little can be done to require their removal.

The amount of coal fines remaining in culm banks around the anthracite region has been estimated to be one billion tons.[48] Culm banks may include coal waste from past mining, but they contain burnable coal and as such they are considered coal reserves for use as fuel. One company in Schuylkill County controls 65 million tons of surveyed culm reserves estimated to contain 16 million tons of coal when cleaned, as well as another 85 million tons of culm reserves that have not been surveyed.[49]

Today, many culm banks are being re-mined for the smaller sizes of coal that can be used in stoker systems. Schuylkill County has five cogeneration plants—power plants that produce electricity as well as steam for heat—that use culm as their primary fuel source. The Wheelabrator Frackville Cogeneration plant may burn as much as 500,000 tons of culm a year.[50]

Before the 1900s, separation of marketable coal from culm and rock was done by hand, by boys ages eight to 12—too young to work in the mines. As the annual production of anthracite grew in the early 1900s, water was increasingly used for cleaning coal and particularly for extracting smaller sizes of marketable coal.

> The sand flotation method uses a mixture of sand and water to clean the coal. The separation of impurities is accomplished by churning the material from the mine in a sand and water mixture. The specific gravity of the coal is less than that of the sand so that the coal can be skimmed off the top;

> the impurities such as slate, on the other hand, have a greater specific gravity than the sand so it sinks to the bottom.[51]

Large amounts of water were used in this process. After marketable sizes of coal were separated from the unusable fines, the coal washing wastewater, fines and all, was often just discharged to nearby streams, the primary means of disposal. All told, this process sent tons of sediment and coal fines to streams. Coal silt was turning the Schuylkill River black as early as 1898.[52]

The deposition of coal fines to the river resulted in abandonment of the upper reaches of the canal beginning as early as 1910. By 1916, so much culm had been discharged to streams in the Schuylkill River's headwaters that it was reported to have "spread over the entire valley bottoms, killing standing timber and all standing vegetation."[53] The main stem Schuylkill River and eleven of its tributaries were contaminated by acid mine drainage; five were "loaded with culm."[54] Deposits of culm in the Schuylkill River below Schuylkill Haven were reported to be six to eight feet deep.[55]

So much coal waste had been discharged to the river over time that an industry sprang up to mine coal from the Schuylkill. Extracting river coal appears to have been a relatively new process in 1901,[56] but by 1907 there were 48 operations mining coal from the Susquehanna and Schuylkill Rivers.[57] By 1907, river coal described as buckwheat-sized was being marketed in Philadelphia and sold for a lower price than buckwheat coal from the mines.[58] In 1916, 60,000 tons of marketable coal were recovered from the Schuylkill.[59] In 1919, the total weight of marketable river coal taken from the Schuylkill was 235,000 tons.[60]

The anthracite coal fields resulted from intense geologic processes. It has been suggested that the folding and faulting gave rise to some of the steepest pitches in the anthracite region, resulting in a more friable coal and a higher percentage of fines.[61, 62] To 1963, total fine waste produced in the coal fields drained by the Schuylkill's headwaters has been estimated at 70 to 80 million tons.[63]

An estimate of 51 million tons of fine waste was produced

through 1928 alone.[64] In 1927, the U.S. Army Corps estimated the total volume of coal waste in the Schuylkill system was 38 million tons,[65] which suggests that a significant portion of the fine waste was going into the river and its tributaries.

In 1940, the Philadelphia Water Department reported that the average coal particle content in the river was 500 parts per million. On March 15th of that year, the coal particle content in the river reached 3,500 parts per million.[66]

In 1945, the estimate for the amount of coal discharged to the river by collieries was still three million cubic yards; the total volume of coal wastes estimated in the river system was 30 million cubic yards. So choked with sediment had the river become that the Schuylkill was described as "too thick to drink and too thin to plow," with writers even finding dark humor in its not being a river at all:

> One chilly day a man stood in the middle of the Schuylkill River in Philadelphia and glumly watched the approach of a police rescue boat. More than cold, more than the water's unpleasant fumes, he felt the bitter humiliation of frustration. Above him towered a bridge, one of the many that carry the nation's third largest city's traffic across the river. A few minutes before, he had been poised on the bridge, a stranger in a strange town, ready to end it all in the water below.
>
> Then he leaped, feet first. Instead of drowning, however, he had simply stuck in the mud, held securely by several feet of it while his head and shoulders were well above the skim of water that ran over the bed of silt. He couldn't move.
>
> The police extricated him from the mud and his predicament, and later sent him on his way, all thoughts of suicide driven from his mind by the shocking discovery that there hadn't been any river there when he had jumped.[67]

But 1945 would mark a turning point for the health of the Schuylkill.

The harm done by carelessly discharging coal silt—the increased cost for maintaining navigation, increased water treatment costs, increased flood losses, and loss of recreational opportunities—was finally becoming too much to bear.

This water [the Schuylkill River] has been dangerous for years.

— *New York Times*, 1885[68]

A Trifling Inconvenience

It would not be unreasonable to ask why the Schuylkill was allowed to become so polluted. By the 1940s, nearly one third of Pennsylvania's 10 million people lived along the river and relied upon it for drinking water.[69] If for no other reason, safeguarding the source of drinking water for so many people would seem reason enough to protect the Schuylkill River. Ancient civilizations, long before the rise of the conservation movement, recognized the benefits of clean water and recommended methods of water treatment.

The City of Philadelphia's experience with water-borne disease made a strong case for preserving the Schuylkill's waters of uncommon purity. Unfortunately for the City, the "solution to pollution is dilution" was for a long time the prevailing belief. Sitting at the bottom of the Schuylkill River watershed, Philadelphia's water supply remains, to this day, at risk from upstream discharges.

The City of Philadelphia and the other communities that relied on the Schuylkill's waters struggled with an increasingly polluted river though the 1800s. Efforts to prevent pollution were met with opposition. In 1868, Alexander Adaire introduced legislation in the Pennsylvania House of Representatives to "preserve the purity of Schuylkill water"[70] by establishing fines on the dumping of waste into the river between Flat Rock Dam and Fairmount Dam. Within one week, manufacturers in the Philadelphia area met to organize opposition to the bill. In less than two weeks, members of the Pennsylvania Senate and House of Representatives received a report prepared by the manufacturers' Committee on Statistics that warned of economic devastation to the region that would be caused by the bill. While acknowledging the need for a clean and plentiful water supply, the manufacturers put the blame for the river's pollution on the sewers of Manayunk, the cemeteries along the river's banks, canal boats, and City streets. In closing, the manufacturers' Committee asked for the legislature to "protect us in the pursuit of our avocations and forbid any interference therewith, on any doubtful experiments to purify the Schuylkill River…"[71]

Polluting the Schuylkill was the cost of doing business, environmental degradation for the benefit of economic development, a trade-off that is still argued today. Pennsylvania's highest court weighed in on the matter in *Pennsylvania Coal Company v. Sanderson*. This case involved the damage to property of Eliza McBriar Sanderson in Scranton, Pennsylvania. Mine water, pumped to the surface from an underground mine operated by the Pennsylvania Coal Company, was discharged to Meadow Brook on the Sanderson property. The acidic mine water killed fish, destroyed vegetation, and corroded machinery.[72] The Sandersons first took legal action against Pennsylvania Coal Company in 1878 in the Court of Common Pleas in Luzerne County, which ruled in favor of Pennsylvania Coal. This decision was appealed to the Pennsylvania Supreme Court which initially reversed the lower court.[73] In all, the case went before the Pennsylvania Supreme Court four times, with Pennsylvania Coal contesting judgments for the Sandersons at each juncture. When the case went back before the Pennsylvania highest court in 1886, the composition of the court had changed.[74] At that time, the court ruled that the damages the Sandersons had suffered were a loss without injury. The Sandersons' property may have been harmed, but that damage did not necessarily allow them legal recourse.[75]

In *Sanderson*, the Pennsylvania Supreme Court ruled that economic benefits were a public good that outweighed "the trifling inconvenience of particular persons" whose water was polluted.[76] In this case, the public good was the economic benefits associated with coal mining; the trifling inconvenience was pollution of Meadow Brook and the damages the Sandersons had suffered. Even in 1886, the *Sanderson* decision was considered contrary to settled law in other states.[77] It has been argued that the Pennsylvania Supreme Court's decision in *Sanderson* applied narrowly to acid mine drainage—"any belief that it gave a green light to pollution is a misconception"[78]—but the decision established a precedent for treating acid mine drainage differently from other forms of water pollution and for decades complicated the regulation of water pollution from the mining of coal.

A decision by the Pennsylvania Supreme Court in 1895, *Hindson v. Markle*, opened the door for regulation of culm under narrow circumstances: coal refuse could not be placed on land in a manner that would allow it to wash into a stream in an ordinary storm or be deposited in a stream in a manner that would cause damage to a lower owner.[79] In July 1896, within months of the *Hindson v. Markle* decision (October 7th, 1895), the City of Philadelphia acted upon guidance from City Solicitor John Kinsey[80] regarding legal action against coal companies discharging coal wastes into the Schuylkill and filed a case against the Philadelphia and Reading Coal and Iron Company, the Lehigh Coal and Navigation Company; the Silver Brook Coal Company, the Broad Mountain Coal Company, the Roberts' Coal Company, and the Stoddard Coal Company.[81]

The City of Philadelphia's case would drag on for many years, but other cases involving culm pollution were resolved more quickly. In 1899, a group of Berks County farmers sued 21 coal companies for damages claimed as a result of agricultural lands destroyed by the deposition of coal silt during high flows.[82] The farmers, who ultimately numbered over 25, settled for $50,000 for the 500 acres that had been damaged by coal silt. The money was to be split among them; the Philadelphia and Reading Coal and Iron Company was responsible for 50 percent of the settlement; Lehigh Coal and Navigation Company would pay 25 percent; and individual operators were responsible for the remaining 25 percent.[83]

A settlement was reached in the City of Philadelphia's case in 1907 with the Philadelphia and Reading Coal and Iron Company and the Lehigh Coal and Navigation Company agreeing to stop dumping culm and mining waste into the river. Unfortunately, the dumping continued.

In the latter half of the 19th century, attitudes about the use, and abuse, of our natural resources were evolving. Even as Pennsylvania's Supreme Court protected abuse by industry, private citizens were beginning to call for protection of natural resources. By the turn of the century, conservationism had become a movement. As president, Theodore Roosevelt made conservation of natural resources a priority. Roosevelt's conservationism was based not upon a belief in the need to protect natural resources for their intrinsic values, but upon the belief that proper management of this country's natural resources was necessary to ensure the best benefit for the American people.

Along with the growth of the conservation movement, a new role for government in the regulation of natural resources was developing. The Purity of Waters Act, passed in 1905 in Pennsylvania, reflects the early view of the role of government in resource management. Authority was given to the Commissioner of Health to regulate new sewage discharges that could be harmful to public health. Recent outbreaks of water-borne disease helped motivate passage of the legislation. Protecting drinking water supplies was the focus of the Act, rather than the regulation of discharges.

Protecting the water supply for communities along the Schuylkill specifically was a likely factor in the passage of the Purity of Waters Act. Within weeks of its passage, the Department of Health began a survey of the sources of the river's pollution. Dr. Seneca Egbert, Dean of the Medico-Chirurgical College of Philadelphia and author of *A Manual of Hygiene and Sanitation*, played a lead role in this study.[84] Dr. Egbert was not impressed with what he observed.

> At the starting point of the trip in Reading, Dr. Egbert says the canal between the Schuylkill and that city was offensively polluted, and also discolored by dyestuffs. The Reading sewage filtration plant, he says, is now far below the standard of efficiency claimed for it when it was first installed nine years ago, and he believes because of the inadequacy of the plant part of the sewage of that city is not being treated at the filters at all, but is discharged directly into the canal or the river.[85]

The City of Reading was likely not pleased with Dr. Egbert's assessment. Reading's first sewer plant, constructed in 1895,[86] was the first such treatment plant built in Pennsylvania.[87] Philadelphia did not build its first sewage treatment plant until 1912.[88]

The Purity of Waters Act regulated new sewage discharges, but the Commissioner of Health was given the power to order the stoppage of existing sewage discharges found to be "injurious to the public health." With that in mind, the growing City of Reading's response to Dr. Egbert's study was to take positive action. Fritz's Island was acquired in order for the City to expand its sewer plant.[89] Reading then became the first municipality in the U.S. to install a trickling filter, a secondary sewage treatment process, in 1907.[90]

Reading's aggressive response was not the norm, nor had it come cheaply; the upgrade of Reading's sewage treatment plant cost $4 million (over $90 million in 2012 dollars).[91] Other communities simply didn't have the money.[92] Moreover, mine drainage and tannery waste—businesses that at the time had strong political influence—were specifically exempted from the 1905 law.[93]

Ultimately, the Purity of Waters Act did little to stop any harmful discharges to Pennsylvania's waters; the Act had no real teeth. Perhaps Grover Cleveland Ladner's assessment best sums up the impact of the Purity of Waters Act:

> Why should millions of dollars of taxpayers' money be spent to clean up streams which industry continued to use as private sewers, was the natural question which officials asked. Thus we had the formation of the vicious circle; the industries and municipalities each saying to the other "you clean up first," with the result that neither performed their duty.[94]

When Ladner spoke those words in 1929, he was Special Counsel for the City of Philadelphia in charge of Schuylkill River pollution litigation.[95] A native Philadelphian, Ladner had first-hand knowledge of the state of the Schuylkill River. He was also an ardent conservationist, active in the Izaak Walton League locally and nationally, and he would go on to help found the Pennsylvania Federation of Sportsmen in 1932.

The next regulatory attempt to stop stream pollution was the Anthracite Culm Act passed in 1913. But this legislation, which only applied to anthracite coal waste being discharged to streams or deposited along streambanks where it might easily wash into streams,[96] simply echoed the Pennsylvania Supreme Court's *Hindson* decision from 18 years earlier. The Act again exempted mine drainage from regulation, and no state agency was charged with the Act's enforcement powers. Still the Act was challenged in court and found to be unconstitutional in 1917 on the grounds that the title of the Act, *An Act to preserve the purity of waters of the State for the protection of public health and property,* did not expressly state its purpose and the application of the Act would have created inequalities between anthracite and bituminous[97] coal mining operations.[98]

Also passed in 1913 was the State Inventory Act which directed the Pennsylvania Water Supply Commission to undertake an inventory of Pennsylvania's water resources. A thorough ten-part report, aptly titled *Water Resources Inventory Report*, was published by the Water Supply Commission in 1916. In a section titled *Culm in the Streams of the Anthracite Region,* the Water Supply Commission did not mince words in its assessment of the impact of mining:

> The contamination of the streams in the coal region has been in progress for more than fifty years, and it is estimated that there are now six hundred and sixty miles of creeks and small streams which should be available for water supply but which are rendered useless for domestic and manufacturing purposes by culm and sulfur water from the mines.[99]

The Water Supply Commission went on to state that it was probable that the Schuylkill was so negatively impacted that its waters would not be fit for use for 150 years. In light of the mining impact, the report recommended enforcement of the Anthracite Culm Act. This report also planted the seed for the Schuylkill cleanup as it suggests that "to restore the river channels to their original carrying capacity, immense amounts of mine waste would have to be dredged from pools, eddies and the slackwater above dams."[100]

Despite this damning assessment by the Water Supply Commission, more stringent regulation of water pollution would have to wait until 1923 and the creation of the Sanitary Water Board within the Department of Health. The intent of the Administrative Reorganization Act of 1923 was to combine in one administrative body the pollution control powers that had previously existed among separate government entities. In addition, the Sanitary Water Board was tasked with classifying all of Pennsylvania's waters into three categories: Class A, or unpolluted streams; Class B, or streams that may be somewhat polluted but could be reclaimed; and Class C, or streams so polluted that restoration was considered impossible. Not surprising, given the Water Supply Commission's 1916 assessment, the Sanitary Water Board designated the Schuylkill River as Class C.

In 1927, the U.S. Army Corps of Engineers estimated that accumulated culm deposits in the river totaled 38 million tons.[101] In 1930, a deep-sea diver who had been contracted to obtain rock samples from the bed of the river in preparation for construction of a new Market Street bridge pronounced the Schuylkill "the dirtiest I ever dived into."[102]

Not everyone was resigned to the Schuylkill River being a lost cause. Sportsmen, conservationists like Grover Ladner, and communities that relied on the Schuylkill for their water supply continued to push for greater regulation of water pollution. It was likely Ladner's private efforts in support of clean streams that earned him the position as Special Counsel for the City of Philadelphia in charge of Schuylkill River pollution litigation in 1928. In this capacity, Ladner pursued polluters in the Philadelphia area and advocated for tough pollution control legislation that would give district attorneys and city solicitors powers to prosecute polluters in the name of the Commonwealth.

Ladner recognized that broad support was needed to stop stream pollution. He took his message to upstream communities that also knew well the problems of the polluted river. In 1933, Ladner spoke eloquently to a Reading Rotary group. His speech was later reprinted in the *Reading Eagle*:

> And now, what has the Schuylkill become? Look at it. It is an offense to the sight and a stench to the nostrils; a fearful mixture of pickling acids, phenol and tar acids, wool scourings, filthy wash water from laundries, bleacheries and dye plants, slaughter house offal, paper mill waste, oil scum and sewage, all liberally thickened with coal culm.
>
> To those of you whose love of outdoors developed to such an extent that your heart aches when you see a polluted stream or a devastated hill top, I need say nothing more. You realize without further argument that something must be done. Take, therefore, your stand with us who aim to make the outdoors cleaner, better and more alive with the pulse of nature.[103]

In 1935, Ladner moved on from his position with the City of Philadelphia to a position as Deputy Attorney General with the Commonwealth. As Deputy Attorney General, he is widely credited with drafting the legislation that is known today as the Clean Streams Law, referred to in 1937 as the Larue Bill, for its sponsor, Berks County representative Mahlon F. Larue, an active sportsman.

The Clean Streams Law, which passed the Pennsylvania Senate by 35-0 and the House by 204-0,[104] was signed by Governor George H. Earle in June 1937 and became effective that September. The scope of this regulation, which remains at the heart of Pennsylvania's regulation of pollution discharges today, moved well beyond prior legislation by requiring protection of aquatic life. The law defined pollution as:

> noxious and deleterious substances rendering unclean the waters of the Commonwealth to the extent of being harmful or inimical to the public health, or to animal or aquatic life, or to the use of such waters for domestic water supply, or industrial purposes, or for recreation.[105]

It provided for the control of sewage discharges and eliminated the exemption for municipal sewer systems that had been included in the Purity of Waters Act.

Although the Clean Streams Law placed a priority on protecting "now clean waters of the Commonwealth," it did not require that polluted streams be restored to a clean condition. And, bad news for the Schuylkill, already polluted streams would be sacrificed to preserve the health of clean streams.

> In the way of prevention, existing laws should be amended to provide that no unpolluted waters may be polluted by acid mine water without a State permit being first granted and no such permit should be granted in any case where it should prove to be reasonably practical to pump acid waters into nearby streams already polluted.[106]

Moreover the Clean Stream Law included exemptions for both coal silt and acid mine drainage, but these exemptions were qualified; they should be permitted only until solutions could be found to deal with these problems.

Ladner explained the exemption for coal silt as a political necessity, but he believed the Sanitary Water Board would soon undertake the called-for study and find that silt could be regulated and removed from mine discharges:

> The House and the sponsor of the Bill, accepted this amendment, rather than risk the Bill failing in the last days of the Session, and in doing so were most wise because in the last analysis it is harmless. Adequate, reasonable and practical means are now known for removing silt and culm. This much was admitted by the spokesman of the mining interests at the House Committee hearing. He stated his company (the largest in the anthracite field) now removes the solids from the silt water, and does so at a profit, for the fine coal thus removed has a very ready market. The Sanitary Water Board can quickly find, therefore, that practical means for removing the same are now known.[107]

Ladner's hopes for the Clean Streams Law would not soon be realized. While the Sanitary Water Board undertook studies of coal silt, culm continued to choke the Schuylkill. In 1941, four pieces of apparatus owned by the Leesport and Goodwill Fire Companies were damaged by water pulled from the Schuylkill River during an attempt to fight a barn fire in rural Berks County.[108]

Neither was the problem of mine drainage solved. In 1941, plans to address this problem included a 36-mile long tunnel draining underground mines in the Schuylkill's headwaters. As proposed, the tunnel would receive acid mine drainage from mines in the area from Ashland to New Boston and from Frackville to Pottsville and discharge it 12 miles above Reading. The plan was touted as potentially saving collieries millions of dollars in pumping costs every year. Ladner, who had been appointed to the Orphans Court of Philadelphia, continued advocating for clean streams as head of the Schuylkill River Valley Restoration Association. Opposed by this and other conservation groups as well as private citizens and communities along the river, the plan did not move forward.[109]

With rationing on the home front and an increased demand for coal during World War II, little progress was made to address the problems of mine drainage and coal silt in the early 1940s. But in 1943 the City of Philadelphia sought to reopen its 1896 legal action against the collieries discharging coal silt into the river. The City asked the Pennsylvania Supreme Court's permission to add the names of 22 coal companies that had not existed at the time of the original action.[110] In addition, a number of communities along the river including Reading, Pottstown, Phoenixville, and Norristown were seeking to join the suit.[111]

Pennsylvania Supreme Court Chief Justice George W. Maxey, as reported in the *Reading Eagle*, seemed skeptical of the City's action, predicting the City "eventually will find it cheaper to tap streams of the Pocono Mountains for its water supply than attempt to clean up the river." Maxey also took issue with the City's cost estimates for cleaning up the river (between $10 million and $15 million, and an additional $1.5 million to $2 million to prevent silt discharge in the future). Maxey pegged the cost of a cleanup at $50 million, but in his view it would be money poorly spent.[112]

> No court order, [sic] installation of desilting devices, he claimed "could prevent nature and heavy rains from forever pouring silt and other deleterious material into the river.[113]

The Pennsylvania Supreme Court rejected the request of those communities seeking to intervene. It also denied the City's request to add the new coal companies to the suit.[114] Ultimately, the Pennsylvania Supreme Court refused to take jurisdiction of Philadelphia's suit, ruling that the Court of Common Pleas was the proper venue, but the Court did allow the City to sue individuals involved in bootleg coal operations.[115]

In October 1943, within weeks of the decision by the Pennsylvania Supreme Court, the City of Philadelphia took its suit to the Court of Common Pleas.[116] The defendant coal companies objected, saying the City had waited too long to reopen the case begun in 1896. Pennsylvania Attorney General Duff petitioned for the Commonwealth to become a co-complainant to the City's suit.[117] In March 1944, Judge Joseph L. Kun overruled the objections of the coal companies and cleared the way for the City to pursue its action against the coal companies.[118] The tide had begun to turn against the careless discharge of coal waste to our rivers.

At this time it was estimated by the U.S. Army Corps of Engineers that approximately three million tons of coal wastes were being dumped in the Schuylkill River each year.[119] By 1944, it was reported that nearly half of the material dredged from the tidal Schuylkill was mine waste.[120] Traces of culm were found in the Delaware River channel 10 miles above and 31 miles below the confluence with the Schuylkill. The volume of coal silt in the Schuylkill was hindering navigation, and, during war time, this raised security concerns.

But even as the war effort was winding down in 1945, change was coming to pollution control in Pennsylvania. Conservation was popular with Pennsylvania voters. On May 8th, the Allies accepted the unconditional surrender of Nazi Germany; war in Europe was over. On May 9th, Governor Edward Martin signed an amendment to the Clean Streams Law known as the Brunner Bill for its sponsor, Charles H. Brunner, Jr., a Montgomery County Republican and advocate for the Schuylkill River. The Brunner Bill, reportedly drafted by Attorney General Duff, finally removed the exemption on the regulation of the discharge of coal silt. The Brunner Bill, also known as Act 177, passed the Pennsylvania Senate 43-6 and the House 178-17.[121]

Although its signing didn't receive the same publicity as the Brunner Bill, Governor Martin signed another piece of legislation shortly after the Brunner Bill, P.L. 1383, No. 441, entitled *Prohibiting Pollution of the Schuylkill River*. P.L. 1383 passed the Pennsylvania Senate 47-1 and the House 195-0.[122] This piece of legislation would become known as the Schuylkill River Desilting Act,[123] and it would make all the difference.

[T]here are many who still haven't found out that pure streams are necessary in Pennsylvania, not only in order that we may live but also that the people of Pennsylvania may properly make a living—that water is important in the daily life of us all.

— Attorney General James H. Duff, 1946[124]

James Henderson Duff

James Henderson Duff deserves his own book. The impacts of Duff's efforts, as attorney general, governor, and senator, on behalf of Pennsylvania and Pennsylvanians continue to be felt today. But, much like the river cleanup that was undertaken by his administration when he was governor, Jim Duff has not gotten the recognition he deserves.

When looking for insight into why and how the Schuylkill cleanup was finally undertaken, Jim Duff commands attention, much as he did on Pennsylvania's political stage from the early 1940s to the late 1950s. But a closer look at Duff finds an unlikely politician.

James Henderson Duff, born in 1883, was the oldest of four children born to Margaret Martin and Joseph Miller Duff, a Presbyterian minister, in Mansfield (now Carnegie), Allegheny County. The Duffs were part of a close but extended family that would gather at the family farm (in what is now Murrysville) that had belonged to his grandfather and namesake, Dr. James Henderson Duff.

Duff had thought to become a doctor like his grandfather, but the recognition he received for his public speaking ability while an undergraduate at Princeton University turned Duff to a career in law. When he was chosen to be one of only four speakers at a speaking contest marking Washington's Birthday, he chose civic duty as his topic and argued that dishonesty, impurity, and luxury eat out the heart of a great nation.[125] Woodrow Wilson was among his professors and influences at Princeton.

He graduated from Princeton in 1904 and began his study of law at the University of Pennsylvania, where he was on the staff of the *American Law Register*.[126] But with his younger brother George Morgan Duff already at Princeton in 1906 and Joseph Miller Duff, Jr. soon to follow in his footsteps, Duff returned home to help his family and graduated from the University of Pittsburgh Law School in 1907. Duff's time at the University of Pennsylvania Law School overlapped with that of Grover Ladner who graduated in 1906.

Among the Duff cousins was Harriett "Hattie" Duff who married John MacFarlane Phillips in 1906. Phillips, an engineer and founder of Phillips Mine Supply Company, was a conservationist in the mold of Theodore Roosevelt. Phillips counted Roosevelt, Gifford Pinchot, and other leaders of the early conservation movement among his friends. He served on the Pennsylvania Game Commission from 1905 until 1924, helped preserve Pennsylvania's first game lands, was among the organizers of the Pennsylvania Federation of Sportsmen's Clubs, and is credited with helping to establish the first Boy Scout troop in Pennsylvania.[127] Phillips was more than 20 years Duff's senior, but in this close knit family, he and his acquaintances were likely influences on the younger man.

Duff married Jean Taylor in 1909. Their only son, John Taylor Duff, died in infancy, but Jim and Jean's home was open to their extended family and at times would include nieces, nephews, and cousins as well.

For 35 years after he graduated from law school, Jim Duff was primarily an attorney in private practice. In addition to his law practice, Duff was a sometime oilman, sometime developer. His business dealings prospered in the 1920s, but fell with the stock market crash leaving him with financial obligations exceeding $100,000 that Duff paid off over 10 years.[128]

Evidence of an interest in politics became apparent early in his career. In 1912, Duff was an elector for Roosevelt. He was a delegate to the Republican National Conventions in 1932, 1936, and 1940 (and would be a delegate in 1948, 1952, and 1956 as well). In 1934, he managed the campaign for governor of his friend, Charles J. Mangiotti. But prior to 1942, the only public office Duff had held was solicitor for the Borough of Carnegie where he lived.

In 1942, when Senator James J. Davis threw his hat in the ring as a Republican candidate for governor, Duff vocally opposed him and suggested he might run against Davis himself. Instead, he ran the gubernatorial campaign of his friend, Edward Martin. When Martin was elected, Duff served first on his transition team and was then appointed Attorney General.

As Attorney General, Duff did something that no one had done to date. He pushed for enforcement of the 1937 Clean Streams Law to prevent the discharge of pollutants into Pennsylvania's streams. In 1944, when the Sanitary Water Board requested guidance from the Attorney General regarding its authority to order treatment of sewage and industrial waste, the opinion of his office underscored the power of the board:

> We are of the opinion that the board may adopt a policy, and regulations to effectuate it, which would require the treatment of sewage and industrial wastes to a specified degree before permitting their discharge into the waters of the Commonwealth, and that the degree or nature of treatment of such wastes may be varied reach by reach of the stream in accordance with existing conditions, so long as these variations are reasonable and practicable.[129]

When the Sanitary Water Board requested guidance on its powers to partially remove the exemption that related to the discharge of coal silt, the opinion from his office urged action:

> The board desires to know, therefore, whether it can declare a limited suspension of the aforesaid exemption of mine drainage from the prohibition against the discharge of industrial wastes into streams, and specify the extent to which such removal of coal mine solids is practicable.
>
> We have no hesitation in concluding that the board has such power and authority. To hold otherwise would be to say that because all mine pollution could not be successfully eliminated at one fell stroke, it should all be tolerated until that becomes possible.[130]

Within days of the guidance being provided, Grover Ladner was calling for Governor Martin to fire the members of the Sanitary Water Board if they did not stop the discharge of pollution to the Schuylkill.[131]

Duff was credited with drafting the Brunner Bill, the 1945

amendment to the Clean Streams Law that officially closed the loophole exempting coal waste discharges from regulation. And when the Sanitary Water Board contemplated continuing to allow the discharge of untreated sewage and industrial waste to the Schuylkill because the river was already degraded by mine drainage, Duff pushed the Board to change its policy.[132]

Duff's official papers show him to be an avid reader. As Attorney General, he carried on correspondence with people who might provide new information on how to combat pollution.

Stream cleanup was a priority for Governor Martin with Duff considered the driving force behind the popular stream cleanup program. When Duff ran for governor after Martin, he campaigned on a pledge to finish what had been started during Martin's administration.

> "No one need have any doubt of my intense interest in the conservation problem in Pennsylvania and of my determination to continue vigorously to do everything in my power to secure the right kind of results of permanent benefit to the people of the Commonwealth," he said.
>
> "In fact, had it not been for the challenge offered by this situation I would not have permitted my name to have been advanced as a candidate for the governorship because I felt the arduous responsibilities of the attorney generalship during the war years might have been public service enough."[133]

Governor Martin opted to run for the U.S. Senate after his term as governor.[134] Duff was handpicked by Martin as the Republican candidate to succeed him as governor in 1946, a selection that was generally supported by others in the party. Duff was popular with voters and was elected by the second largest margin of victory to that time, over 500,000 votes. To date, only Bob Casey, Sr.,(1990), Ed Rendell (2006), Tom Ridge (2002), and John S. Fisher (1926) enjoyed larger margins of victory.[135,136]

Perhaps Martin's Republican colleagues should have recalled Duff's early progressive spirit. If they had, they might not have been as surprised by the actions he would take once elected. For decades, Pennsylvania politics had been dominated by conservative Republican Joseph Grundy, the Bristol-based textile manufacturer and head of the Pennsylvania Manufacturers Association. Jim Duff came to oppose Joe Grundy and his political machine which Duff was known to refer to as "government by a few, for the benefit of a few, at public expense." Duff believed government should do for people what they could not do for themselves, which included the conservation and restoration of natural resources.

Duff was sworn in as governor on January 21st, 1947, his 64th birthday. An outdoorsman who stood six-feet tall, Duff's vitality belied his age as did the activities he undertook while governor.

As governor, Duff pushed programs to clean up streams, construct municipal sewage treatment plans, and build roads and expand turnpike construction. He asked for bonuses for Pennsylvanians who had served in the military during the war. He raised teachers' salaries and increased spending for mental health. Duff's programs were paid for by continuing the manufacturers' tax, doubling taxes on cigarettes and malt beverages, increasing taxes on gasoline, and taxing soda at one cent per 12 ounces of soda.[137] And during his administration, the "Tax Anything Law" was passed which allowed municipalities to raise money by taxing anything the Commonwealth didn't.

Both as Attorney General and as Governor, Duff frequently spoke to citizens' groups and sportsmen's clubs, urging public support for stream cleanup efforts. Few records of the talks he gave can be found among his official papers; however, numerous requests for copies of his speeches are included. He wrote his own speeches, but, as it has been said that Duff often waited until the last minute to prepare these talks (R. Phillips, personal communication, 16 May 2011), he may have extemporized.

After serving as governor, Duff ran for and was elected to the U.S. Senate. Duff was instrumental in securing Dwight Eisenhower's candidacy as the Republican nominee for president in 1952. As Senator, he encouraged President Eisenhower to consider setting up cancer research facilities associated with universities and hospitals; he was concerned about health care of low income people; and he helped establish the President's Physical Fitness Test.

However, Duff does not appear to have enjoyed being a senator and said he only ran for re-election in 1956 because Eisenhower asked him to. But he had made enemies in Pennsylvania politics, and, after a brutal campaign, he was defeated by Joseph S. Clark, Jr.

Duff always said his stream cleanup efforts were the accomplishment for which he thought he would be most remembered and indeed they were prominently reported among his achievements when he passed away in Washington, D.C., on December 20th, 1969.

Duff was an avid outdoorsman who claimed he could identify any tree or rock formation in Pennsylvania. He was a gardener and believed in planting trees. He loved dogs almost as much as he loved a good political fight when he thought he was right. He closed the loophole exempting coal silt from the Clean Streams Law, and his legacy was capped by the Schuylkill cleanup, the first major river restoration undertaken by a government agency in the U.S. It's time that both Duff and the cleanup get the recognition they deserve.

"Since the contemplated action is manifestly in the public interest it is felt that the vast majority of those responsible for pollution will collaborate with the state in bringing about the most desirable result.

"However, the state is under the obligation to bring about results and as to those refusing voluntary collaboration there will be no option but legal process."

— Attorney General James H. Duff, 1944[138]

An Actionable Wrong

Before beginning a cleanup of rivers that have suffered decades of abuse, a wise first course of action would be to stop the very discharges that caused those rivers to be polluted. The Sanitary Water Board began taking steps to address industrial and municipal discharges to Pennsylvania's waterways after receiving guidance from the Attorney General's office in early 1944. Those first steps included public hearings so industries and municipalities would understand what was expected of them.[139] These hearings were held during the summer of 1944.[140] But the Sanitary Water Board didn't begin ordering treatment of discharges immediately after the hearings; it first "strongly urged that municipalities and industries undertake the preparation of plans in order to be prepared for the day when the war ceases."[141]

In late 1944 and early 1945, the Sanitary Water Board began issuing orders directing industries and municipalities to prepare plans for post-war sewage treatment works, but Attorney General Duff may have felt the Board was moving too cautiously. As the first notices were being sent to municipalities and industries, the Attorney General's office released a statement reiterating the need for cooperation by cities and towns, mines and industry, but added that "the state is under the obligation to bring about results and as to those refusing voluntary collaboration there will be no option but legal process."[142]

As the Sanitary Water Board finally moved to order construction of treatment plants and set deadlines for completion of facilities,[143] some municipalities and industries balked at the costs. Such cases were referred to Attorney General Duff for potential enforcement action, a move that appears to have been effective at bringing about compliance with treatment orders for sewage and industrial discharges.[144]

With the passage of the Brunner Bill amending the Clean Streams Law, the Sanitary Water Board could also begin ordering collieries and washeries to prevent coal silt from being washed into the river. The Sanitary Water Board's progress could be tracked in

"Pennsylvania's Anti-Pollution Progress," a recurring column that appeared in the *Pennsylvania Angler* during the late 1940s that followed cleanup efforts on the Schuylkill and other Pennsylvania rivers.

But how do you remove the tons of coal culm that had been washed into the river for over a hundred years? Above Reading, the deposits of coal silt were so deep that the form and function of the Schuylkill River had been altered considerably.

> We recall that scarcely two years ago there was no river bed to carry off flood waters from the Schuylkill. At most locations, coal silt had accumulated in piles as high as twenty-six feet deep, with three feet of normal water flow above![145]

Dredging coal out of the river was nothing new. Marketable coal had been mined from the Schuylkill River since the early 1900s. River coal was touted as a valuable asset to the towns along the river for the cheap fuel it provided.[146] A river coal industry, mining the coal silt deposited in the river, existed on the Schuylkill. The Schuylkill Haven Drifted Coal Company boasted of operating almost continuously for four years in an area of the river measuring just 4,000 square feet.[147] In 1919, 235,000 tons of marketable river coal was dredged from the Schuylkill.[148] One river coal business operating in the Stoudt's Ferry area was able to reclaim 100 tons of No. 4 and No 5 buckwheat coal every day over a nine month period in 1947.[149] But with the volume of coal silt washed into the river every year estimated to be at least two million tons, [150] the Schuylkill's river coal industry was leaving far more coal in the river than it was removing.

The coal removed from the Schuylkill was primarily dredged from the riverbed using pumps or buckets and then piped or brought to shore for cleaning.[151] The river coal industry was also likely washing coal fines back into the river as it cleaned the dredged material to extract marketable sizes of coal.

The idea of cleaning up the Schuylkill by removing coal culm drew upon the model used by the river coal dredging operations and, before them, by the Schuylkill Navigation system. Proposals for large scale dredging of the river dated at least to 1916,[152] but a significant barrier to the implementation of any dredging plan was the continued discharge of coal wastes by collieries and washeries. The cost of a cleanup, estimated in the millions, as well as who should bear the burden of that cost, also remained a barrier. The federal government had been involved in the management of the tidal Schuylkill since 1870[153] and many felt it should have a role in cleaning up the Schuylkill. However, the federal government's interests were in maintaining the tidal channel and it didn't feel the need to expend funds for dredging further upriver.[154] Controlling the discharge of coal silt was Pennsylvania's problem.

As of 1930, the City of Philadelphia had taken responsibility for dredging 300,000 cubic yards of spoils from the river every year.[155] By 1935, that effort to maintain a navigable tidal channel cost $750,000 annually.[156] By 1945, the City's annual dredging commitment was inadequate to maintain the tidal channel.[157] As the lower Schuylkill became filled with coal waste, it was becoming more difficult for the federal government to avoid the problem.

A number of surveys had been undertaken to assess the volume of coal silt in the river over the years, including surveys by the Water Supply Commission and the Sanitary Water Board and even by individuals. In 1927, H.W. Althouse, a civil and mining engineer and geologist, reported that in the reach of the river from Schuylkill Haven to Reading he had observed 127 silt and culm flats averaging 32 feet in width, 228 feet in length and up to 10 feet in depth.[158]

Another man who studied the volume of coal silt in the river was Frederick H. Dechant, a consulting engineer based in the Reading area who knew the river well. Dechant was a Berks County native and son of William H. Dechant, a civil engineer[159] who also had advocated for cleaning up the Schuylkill. A member of the Pollution Committee of the Reading Chamber of Commerce, the younger Dechant had studied the Schuylkill extensively and had gathered research on restoring streams.[160,161]

In 1935, when the U.S. Army Corps of Engineers was persuaded to undertake a study of the coal silt in the Schuylkill River, Dechant assisted.[162] The study moved forward at this time in part because of funding that came from the Works Progress Administration, a jobs program that was part of Franklin D. Roosevelt's New Deal. In addition to the survey work, the project involved building walls around culm banks to prevent coal silt from washing into the river. The survey, which cost nearly $200,000,[163] was expanded to consider the entire watershed and looked at how to prevent coal from entering the river.

The final report of the survey estimated that 22 million cubic yards of culm filled the river[164] and it included recommendations of actions to improve the condition of the Schuylkill: scouring, draining, and removing encroachments to the river channel,[165] work that would provide jobs for thousands of men.[166]

But after two years of study, the position that the federal government's interest was limited to the Schuylkill's tidal channel still held. Reportedly, E.B. Sandelands, the engineer who had overseen the survey, and Col. John C. H. Lee, Commander of the U.S. Army Corps' Philadelphia District, recommended that federal funding be provided to undertake the culm removal, but the federal government wasn't interested.[167]

Efforts to encourage the federal government to play a role in cleaning up the Schuylkill continued for a time[168] and then took a back seat to the war effort. But as World War II wound down and Attorney General Duff's war on river pollution heated up, a new player stepped into the discussion of how to clean up the Schuylkill River. The Interstate Commission on the Delaware River Basin, or INCODEL, was an advisory committee created in 1936 with representation from Delaware, New Jersey, New York, and Pennsylvania. Cleaning up stream pollution was among INCODEL's priorities[169] and in October 1943 INCODEL put forward a plan for cleaning up the Schuylkill:[170]

- The discharge of mine wastes into the river would be stopped;
- Pennsylvania would bear the cost for dredging the Schuylkill above Norristown;

- Pennsylvania would finance a desilting basin at Auburn;[171]
- The federal government would bear the cost for dredging undertaken by the U.S. Army Corps of Engineers between Norristown and Philadelphia; and
- Pennsylvania's Sanitary Water Board would require all municipalities to install necessary collection and treatment facilities.

At a 1944 conference that included federal, state, and local officials, citizens' groups, and a mining company, INCODEL secured consensus on these elements as an action plan.[172] Indeed, elements like those in the INCODEL proposal would make their way into the final plan that would be enacted to clean up the river.

But in August 1943, even before INCODEL put forward its river cleanup plan, Governor Martin had established a Post-War Planning Commission which included Attorney General Duff. No surprise then that the Commission made cleaning up Pennsylvania's streams a priority. For the City of Philadelphia and clean streams advocates like Grover Ladner, momentum finally seemed to be going their way and building toward real action. Governor Martin's comments the next year—"I'm not going to recommend funds for any particular stream"[173]— may have raised some concerns, but the passage of the Brunner Bill and the Schuylkill River Desilting Act in 1945 marked a turning point. Real cleanup was coming to the Schuylkill River.

The Schuylkill River Desilting Act, P.L. 1383, No. 441, entitled *Prohibiting Pollution of the Schuylkill River*, specifically authorized the Water and Power Resources Board of the Department of Forests and Waters to:

- "Clean out, widen, alter, dredge, deepen or change the course, current or channel" of the Schuylkill River;
- Make surveys and prepare plans;
- Acquire land, including by condemnation;
- Enter into contracts; and
- Enter into agreements with the federal government as well as local governments.

In addition, $5 million was appropriated to the Schuylkill River

Desilting Fund.

The federal government may have remained skeptical that Pennsylvania would really make a break from past practices.[174] It too signed on to the proposed cleanup program by December 1945,[175] but that participation came with conditions:

- The discharge of mine and industrial wastes into the Schuylkill would be stopped;
- Desilting pools would be constructed to catch coal wastes eroding from culm piles;
- Fifty percent of culm from the reach of the river between Auburn and Norristown would be removed;
- Assurance that the remaining 50 percent of culm in this reach would be removed; and
- Land, easements, and access for construction of the project would be provided.

The federal government agreed that once Pennsylvania had removed 50 percent of the coal silt in the 98 miles of the river above Norristown, the U.S. Army Corps of Engineers would clean up the reach of the river from Norristown to Fairmount Dam. Governor Martin signed off on these conditions in November 1945 and with that the Schuylkill River Project, Pennsylvania's first state-federal joint venture, was officially underway.

The unhappy river has no channel, only flat beds of silt backed up behind dams.

— Bill Wolf, 1949[176]

The Worst First

The pieces had finally all fallen into place to begin a cleanup of the Schuylkill, regarded as Pennsylvania's—if not this country's—dirtiest river. But those looking for signs that the Schuylkill River Project was underway in 1946 had little to console them. In 1946 and 1947 shortages—meat, wheat, paper, coal, fuel oil, lead, and steel—were still a fact of life, and this limited the work that could be done to clean up the river.

Governor Duff, who had made the Schuylkill River Project a priority, was sworn in on January 21st 1947. Expectations were for him to push the project aggressively.[177] As governor, Duff would not be able to maintain the direct role he had enjoyed as attorney general. He needed an able administrator sympathetic to his concern about river pollution. For secretary of the Department of Forests and Waters, the man who would be responsible for the project, Duff tapped retired Admiral Milo F. Draemel. As Commandant of the Fourth Naval District and Philadelphia Naval Yard from 1942 to 1946, Draemel had first-hand knowledge of the polluted Schuylkill.

Under Draemel's leadership, the Water and Power Resources Board entered into a contract with four engineering firms in June 1947. These engineering firms, Harris and Dechant; Day and Zimmerman, Inc.; Albright and Friel, Inc.; and Justin and Courtney, would become known as the Schuylkill River Project Engineers, and they were given a four-year contract: just four years to reverse the damage that had been done to the river over decades.

Each firm came to the project with a different expertise and each was responsible for a different part of the Schuylkill cleanup. Harris and Dechant took on oversight of dredging, dredge equipment, and channel clearing. Albright and Friel, Inc., and Justin and Courtney shared responsibilities for the dams and desilting pools.[178,179] Day and Zimmerman, Inc., handled the general management for the entire project.

Representatives of each firm comprised an executive committee, led by Frederick Hagman Dechant, that directed planning, preparation of contracts and specifications, and oversight of subcontracts. As a Reading native, Dechant, of Harris and Dechant, had the most extensive experience with the Schuylkill River. A graduate of the University of Pennsylvania and a Navy veteran, he had consulted on the 1935 assessment of the Schuylkill River by the U.S. Army Corps of Engineers. As a civil engineer, Dechant had patented a process for using waste coal for energy generation.[180]

Other members of the executive committee included Francis De Sales Friel, Albright and Friel; Joel Bates Justin and Neville C. Courtney, Justin and Courtney; and George Schobinger and Harry A. Reed, Day and Zimmerman.

Friel, a Drexel graduate, had served with the U.S. Army Corps of Engineers during World War I.[181] He worked for the Pennsylvania Department of Health before leaving to join the firm of Albright and Mebus (which would become Albright and Friel). Friel was an engineer with a national reputation and he had consulted extensively on water and sewer projects around the region. Justin, of Justin and Courtney, was a graduate of Cornell University. Justin and Courtney had been established by Joel De Witt Justin, a well-known hydraulic engineer and the father of Joel Bates Justin. The younger Justin had experience with dam construction and operations from his work with the Tennessee Valley Authority and the Appalachian Electric Power Company. He was one of the youngest of the Schuylkill River Project Engineers, as much as 20 years younger than his colleagues. Schobinger had worked for the U.S. Reclamation Service (which would become the U.S. Bureau of Reclamation). A graduate of the University of Chicago and the Massachusetts Institute of Technology, Schobinger had worked on water supply projects at Elephant Butte, New Mexico, and along the Colorado River in Arizona before coming to Philadelphia to work for American International Shipbuilding Company at Hog Island.[182] He was also a co-author of *Business Methods in the Building Field: A Manual of Practice in Documentary Procedure for the Development, Prosecution and Execution of Industrial, Power and Buildings Projects.*

In September 1947, the Schuylkill River Project Engineers submitted a flexible action plan for the Schuylkill River cleanup to the Water and Power Resources Board where it was met with approval. The plan was simple and intended to be modified in response to the changing river conditions likely to be seen during the course of the project:

- Stop discharges of coal wastes and dumping of refuse to the river;
- Use the river's flow to move the coal wastes to locations where they could be removed;
- Move coal silt and culm from the river to impounding basins on the river's banks;
- Construct a desilting pool on the river to trap remaining or future sediments; and
- Remove obstructions and restore the channel's capacity to carry flood waters.[183]

The Sanitary Water Board was responsible for stopping the coal discharges. The Schuylkill River Project Engineers would be responsible for the rest. However, a letter from Dechant to Draemel suggests that at least he, if not all of the Schuylkill River Project Engineers, had their doubts about whether the Sanitary Water Board would be able to accomplish its task.

> Coal mine wastes are characterized as industrial wastes. In fact they are, but consist of two components, the acid mine waters, and the solid portion called "culm".[sic] It is thus with all silting material and solid materials concern [sic] the Water and Power Resources Board because of its duty "to protect and improve stream channels."...
>
> It is believed to be in the best interest of the Commonwealth to separate control of pollution this nature [sic] from the Sanitary Water Board and transfer the control to the Department of Forests and Waters.[184]

Despite Dechant's misgivings, control over the coal waste discharges remained with the Sanitary Water Board which undertook a survey in the Schuylkill's headwaters to identify these operations. In September 1948, the Sanitary Water Board was reporting that 32 of the 56 known collieries in the river's headwaters had operations in place to trap their coal wastes or were nearing completion of their facilities. These 32 coal operations were said to represent 80 percent of total coal production in the region.[185]

With the Sanitary Water Board seeing to the coal wastes, the Water and Power Resources Board and the Schuylkill River Project Engineers could turn their attention to removing coal waste from the river.

Together, Pennsylvania and the federal government proposed to remove an estimated 30 million cubic yards of coal silt from the river. But first, the Water and Power Resources Board needed to acquire access to the river and ownership of land where the coal silt would be placed. In addition to the lands where the impounding basins would be constructed, the Schuylkill River Project Engineers' plan required access to a 40-foot strip of land along both banks for nearly the full length of the river, well over 100 miles.[186] The Water and Power Resources Board had also committed to securing the lands necessary for the federal dredging effort from Norristown to the Schuylkill's confluence with the Delaware. As a result, in 1947, 1948, and even into 1949, extensive effort was spent acquiring land, including the Schuylkill Navigation lands, for the Schuylkill River Project.

Roughly 1,500 acres of land was acquired for the work of the Schuylkill River Project[187] at a total cost of $1,356,759 ($13,982,222.85 in 2012 dollars).[188] When property records were unclear, land surveys were undertaken by registered surveying firms such as Damon and Foster. At times, staff of the Schuylkill River Project Engineers also assisted with land surveys. The long delays in land acquisition resulted in frustration at the highest levels and Secretary Draemel personally pushed the speed of the land acquisition with subordinates.[189] Unfortunately, some of the disputed title issues that caused delays would result in difficult relations for the staff of the Schuylkill River Project with adjoining landowners for years to come.[190]

In all, 55 construction contracts were awarded to 23 contractors by the Schuylkill River Project Engineers.[191] In addition, as many as 25 subcontractors were approved to assist the contractors.[192] Among the first contracts awarded, in October 1947, was the removal of old Schuylkill Navigation dams near the Schuylkill River Gap in order to begin the process of using the gradient of the river to move coal silt downstream.[193]

Once the silt had been moved to the desired locations, the Schuylkill River Project Engineers proposed to dredge it from the river and pump it to impounding basins where it would be dewatered. Construction of individual impounding basins[194] required clearing as much as 100 acres of land; removing top soil; creating the encircling embankments from as much as 450,000 cubic yards of local soil and stone; and installing a waste weir, or drain, allowing the water in the dredged coal slurry to return to the river as the coal silt settled in the basin.[195] The storage capacity of the impounding basins ranged from 380,000 to 2.5 million cubic yards.[196]

Compounding the delays associated with land acquisition was the weather:

> An analysis of precipitation records show an excess recorded at all stations except Pottsville for the 1947-1948 water year,[197] varying by 5 inches at Philadelphia, 12 inches at Pottstown, 4 inches at Reading, and 2 inches at Port Clinton…The following water year, 1948-1949, shows an excess of 7 inches at Philadelphia and nearly normal rainfall at other stations…
>
> The winter of 1947-1948 was exceptionally cold during January, that month being the sixth coldest on record. The river was frozen to a depth of about a foot in many places. The winter of 1948-1949 was, [sic] by contrast unusually warm.[198]

Weather continued to be a factor throughout the Schuylkill River Project. Heavy rains and high river flows would take a toll on both men and machines working to clean up the river.

Many of the impounding basin contracts—which required earth moving to create huge bowl-shaped structures along the river's banks—were completed by the contract deadline or by the date of an approved extension; however, one contractor, S.J. Groves and Sons, fared worse in the weather conditions. The company, a Minnesota-based, heavy construction firm which had a role in the construction of many Interstate highways, was awarded 11 of the 23 impounding basins contracts. Of these eleven contracts, only three were completed by the initial contract deadline. Eight contract extensions were approved, and the company was able to complete work on six more impoundments by the extension date, but they ran past the extended deadline for two basins, at Black Rock and Mingo. The contractor ran past extended deadlines by 18 and 40 days, respectively, and it was fined $50 per day for these delays which were attributed primarily to weather.[199]

Work on the basins didn't always end with completion of construction. During the dredging, the Schuylkill River Project Engineers would have to deal with seepage from the Seyfert basin, below Reading, that polluted groundwater and caused the basements of nearby homes to flood.[200] Further downriver, a portion of the embankment surrounding the Middle Abrams basin collapsed during pumping which required repairs by the dredging contractor. Both issues resulted in increased costs for the respective dredging contracts.[201]

The total cost of the 23 impounding basin contracts was $3,977,194 (more than $40 million in 2012 dollars).[202]

The Schuylkill River Project Engineers planned to use the river's flow to move coal silt to where it could be removed, but coal silt and culm hadn't accumulated only in the river bed. Large amounts of silt had been deposited along the Schuylkill's banks during high flows as well. Some of these deposits were removed and trucked to the impounding basins,[203] but most were pushed back into the river, again to allow its flows to move the silt to locations where dredging was possible.

The shallow, silted Schuylkill complicated dredging plans:

The problem of dredging the river deposits required that dredging equipment should have shallow draft, and low overhead clearances in order to negotiate the channel, and be of the type that could be assembled on separable pontoons. The dredges could be "knocked down" and transported overland, from one dredging station to another, where water depth permitted movement.[204]

As a result, dredging equipment was designed specifically for the Schuylkill River Project. In all, five dredges were built by the American Steel Dredge Company of Fort Wayne, Indiana. The first four dredges ordered were identical—78 feet long, 30 feet wide and seven feet in depth— with hulls consisting of nine pontoons assembled in three rows of three.[205] The dredges were designed to pass under bridges with only 13 feet of clearance by increasing the draft from three feet, two inches to four feet by flooding the six outboard pontoons.[206] The deckhouse, made of sheet-steel panels, measured 65 feet long, 20 feet wide and 10 feet high. Like the hull, the deckhouse could be easily disassembled.[207]

The dredges were equipped with 57-inch enclosed cutterheads[208] with 15-inch suction pipes. The cutterheads were powered by 75 horsepower electric motors; the main dredge pumps were driven by 1,250 horsepower electric motors. Portable substations on shore provided the electricity which was transmitted to these dredges via submarine cables.[209]

The pump capacity was expected to be 400 cubic yards per hour with actual performance achieved of 700 cubic yards per hour[210] with one hitting 1,000 cubic yards per hour.[211] The ladders carrying the cutterheads could be extended to reach 20 feet below the surface of the water.

The fifth dredge ordered, designed specifically for the Tamaqua desilting basin, was smaller than the first four, with a hull was 51 feet long, 26 feet wide and five feet in depth, and was also made by assembling pontoons. The Tamaqua dredge, which was diesel powered, had a ten-inch suction pipe with an eight-inch discharge pipe.[212]

The four identical dredges cost $298,000 each ($2,841,696 in 2012 dollars).[213] The smaller diesel dredge cost $195,355 ($1,726,750 in 2012 dollars).[214]

Even though the contract for the first four dredges was among the first to be awarded, in February 1948, the term of the contract—each of the four dredges constructed, assembled afloat, tested, and accepted by the Commonwealth—was not completed until June 1949.[215] The Tamaqua dredge wasn't ready to go to work on the Little Schuylkill until 1951.

But the Schuylkill River Project Engineers didn't wait for their custom made dredges to be delivered to begin removing coal silt. The first dredging contract was awarded in June 1948. The official launch of the Schuylkill River Project was September 22nd, 1948.

Jim Duff believed in the Schuylkill River Project, but he also understood the importance of public opinion. Three years had gone by since the Schuylkill River Desilting Act had been passed, but not one yard of coal silt had been removed from the river. The official start of the Schuylkill River Project would be no simple ceremony. At invitation from the Governor and Secretary Draemel, as many as 150 people—reporters, politicians, engineers, planners, conservationists, and private citizens—came to the Reading area for this special occasion.

The official launch of the cleanup began with a luncheon at the Wyomissing Club in Reading, followed by a bus tour with stops to see the first dredge launched at Cross Keys as well as nearby impounding basins and the Kernsville Dam under construction.

With so many reporters in attendance, the media-savvy Duff had ensured that the official project launch received wide coverage. The local papers, the *Reading Eagle* and the *Reading Times*, provided extensive coverage of the launch as well as later project work. The Schuylkill River Project had a friend at the *Reading Times*, Editor Herbert C. Kohler. An avid fisherman and clean streams advocate, Kohler had written numerous editorials in support of a river cleanup.

A full color publication, *The Schuylkill River Project: Restoring a Natural Resource to the People of Pennsylvania*, was made available to people upon request. If there was any doubt that Duff intended to make good on his promise to clean up the Schuylkill, the project launch ceremony was designed to dispel it:

> A little further up the river at Cross Keys we saw the first dredge cutting into the muck, loosening the culm, and sucking the dirt and water which is pumped into the impounding basin. We crossed the river to see the silt being spread over the several areas of the basin, where the silt is allowed to settle. The clear water will be drained from on top by means of a concrete weir with a series of flood gates ingeniously arranged for the successively higher water levels.[216]

And with that, Eastern Engineering's dredge "Queen" went to work on the Schuylkill, removing coal silt not for navigation or for profit, but for the first time to restore the river's function.

Eastern Engineering received the lion's share of dredging contracts on the Schuylkill including: Section I, from Kernsville to just above the City of Reading, a distance of roughly 20 miles; Section II, from just above Reading to below Poplar Neck, a distance of roughly eight miles; Section III, from just below Poplar Neck to Pottstown, a distance of roughly 18 miles; and Section IV, from Pottstown to Black Rock Dam, a distance of roughly 15 miles. American Dredging Company received the contract for dredging Section V, from Black Rock Dam to Norristown, a distance of roughly 12.5 miles.[217]

Each of these contracts included work beyond just dredging, such as bulldozing culm along banks back into the river. In some cases, due to the distance from impounding basins, sediments were dredged from upstream areas and discharged further downstream only to be dredged up again and discharged to the impounding basins. Contractor dredges, the "Queen" and the "King," were used in sections I, II, and III. The state-owned dredges, "Berks," "Chester," "Montgomery," and "Schuylkill," were used on sections IV and V.[218]

Dredging contractors were paid by the yard of material dredged.

Soundings of sediment levels were taken before and after dredging to verify the amount of material dredged. At the beginning of the project, the Schuylkill River Project Engineers estimated that 24 million cubic yards of coal silt were in the river from Kernsville to Norristown. The greatest volume sediment per mile was believed to be in Section II, the reach of the river from just above Reading to below Poplar Neck.

As the Schuylkill River Project progressed, the estimate of the volume of sediment that would be removed dropped to 18 million cubic yards, in part due to rain events and high river flows that moved sediments downriver below Norristown where it would be the responsibility of the U.S. Army Corps of Engineers.[219] These estimates of sediments in the river and dredging projections were more than just benchmarks for project success; removal of 50 percent of the coal silt in the river was a trigger for the federal government to begin its cleanup from Norristown to the Schuylkill's confluence with the Delaware.

The Schuylkill River Project Engineers did not provide a precise total of the amount of material dredged from the Schuylkill. Their final estimates and prior year progress reports suggest the total quantity of sediment that was dredged, but a later report provides a different total. At least 16.5 million cubic yards were removed, but a figure of 16.8 million cubic yards was also reported before completion of the official project.[220] A later report indicated that over 17.25 million cubic yards of sediment were removed from the river from Sections I through V.[221]

Eastern Engineering dredged approximately 12.6 million cubic yards of sediment for a total payment of $12,564,049.85. American Dredging Company dredged approximately four million total cubic yards for a total payment of $2,915,180.13.[222]

In the reach from Reading to Norristown, a contract was awarded to the Conduit and Foundation Corporation to construct or repair temporary dams to impound enough water to float the dredges.[223] The temporary dams were constructed at Birdsboro, Douglassville, Pottstown, and Pickering Creek and at the location of the Schuylkill

Navigation's Pawling's and Catfish dams. Eastern Engineering's contract for dredging section IV also included construction and removal of temporary dams at Linfield and Cromby. High flows during the project caused damage to a number of these temporary dams with breaches of both the Birdsboro and Linfield dams that required extensive repairs, adding to the cost of their associated contracts.[224]

The biggest construction elements of the Schuylkill River Project were the desilting pools, impoundments resulting from the construction of three new dams to slow water in the upper parts of the watershed to catch any coal sediment still washing into the river.

It was anticipated that some coal would continue to wash into the river from culm banks and this, together with coal silt that remained in the tributaries of the Schuylkill's headwaters, could continue to move downstream. But coal silt would no longer be coming from collieries and washeries. The Sanitary Water Board reported that the 47 mining operations along the Schuylkill had installed their own settling ponds to trap coal silt and that, as of 1949, they were trapping as much as two million tons of silt annually.[225] Stopping the discharge of coal silt from the collieries and washeries was another benchmark that Pennsylvania had to meet to trigger the federal cleanup below Norristown.

A third benchmark for federal participation was the construction of two dams to form desilting pools on the Schuylkill River. The first dam undertaken to create a desilting pool was the New Kernsville Dam above Hamburg. Work on this dam, referred to locally simply as "Kernsville," began in 1948 and was completed in 1949. The tasks that had to be undertaken before dam construction included not only excavation of the site for dam construction but also the removal of extensive deposits of culm.

Kernsville is a concrete gravity dam; its very weight and structure provide resistance against forces, such as upstream flows and sediment, acting upon it. The dam is 1,100 feet long with a spillway 600 feet long. The height of the dam is 45 feet, but approximately 28 feet of this height is below the level of the riverbed.[226]

The dam was built in two stages with work on the left side (looking downstream) occurring in 1948. The river was diverted around the dam construction by a coffer dam. As construction got underway on the right side of the dam, the river was diverted back through the completed section of the dam.[227]

George Heckman, Hamburg, grew up on the banks of the Schuylkill near the site of the Kernsville Dam. In a June 22nd, 2012, interview, Heckman, who was barely a teenager at the time of the dam's construction, recalled watching the progress of the cleanup and dam construction. Heckman remembered the heavy rains and flooding that occurred during Kernsville's construction. "In the river, they had a barge with a crane on it to lift stone into place," said Heckman. "The cable on the barge snapped. It was like a shot going off. The barge went over the dam and the crane with it. They tried to get it out, but they never did. That crane is still there at the base of the dam," added Heckman.

Weather wasn't the only factor complicating Kernsville's construction. There is a saying that if water is safe to drink, it's suitable for making concrete. Poirier and McLane Corporation, the contractor building Kernsville, was concerned that the Schuylkill's acidic water, with a pH of 5, would weaken the concrete. To compensate, the contractor diverted river water through a settling pond and added lime before the concrete was mixed.[228]

The Kernsville Dam creates a pool over a mile long with a surface area of 54 acres and drains an area of approximately 340 square miles. The impounding basin associated with the Kernsville desilting pool has a capacity of 750,000 cubic yards.[229]

The second and most upstream desilting pool on the Schuylkill River was formed by the construction of the Auburn Dam, another concrete gravity dam. Construction began in 1949 and was completed in 1950. Work on Auburn was also undertaken in two phases with work beginning on the right section (looking downstream) first. The dam is 820 feet long with a spillway 500 feet long. The height of the dam is 46 feet, with approximately 28 feet of this height below the level of the riverbed.[230]

Auburn Dam creates a pool roughly three miles long with a surface area of 186 acres and drains an area of approximately 157 square miles. The impounding basins associated with the Auburn desilting pool have a capacity of 3,350,000 cubic yards.[231]

The final desilting pool created under the Schuylkill River Project was downstream of Tamaqua on the Little Schuylkill River. Instead of constructing another concrete gravity dam to impound water, the Schuylkill River Project Engineers contracted with the John P. Leaming Company to excavate a desilting basin, 800 feet wide, 1,200 feet long, and eight feet below the level of the adjacent river bed. This basin was constructed to the right (looking downstream) of the river channel. The Little Schuylkill was then diverted into the excavated basin, and its original channel filled. About 300 feet below the basin's outlet, where it returned to its channel, a weir was constructed across the river.[232]

Construction on the Tamaqua weir was the last of the three desilting basin projects to get underway in July 1949, but it was completed before the Auburn Dam. The low weir is stone construction and only 92 feet long.[233] In 1962, the height of the Tamaqua weir was raised three feet to increase storage capacity in the desilting pool.[234]

The Tamaqua basin is only 1,200 feet long with a surface area of 20 acres and drains an area of approximately 67 square miles. The impounding basins associated with the Tamaqua desilting pool have a capacity of over one million cubic yards.[235]

In addition to the sediments dredged from the river below Kernsville, approximately 1.4 million more cubic yards of sediment was dredged from the three desilting pools during the official phase of the Schuylkill River Project, bringing the total sediments dredged to very near if not over the Schuylkill River Project Engineers' revised estimate of 18 million cubic yards that needed to be removed from the river above Norristown.[236]

With the completion of the desilting pools, Pennsylvania had achieved all the benchmarks put forward by the federal government to secure its participation:

- Under orders from the Sanitary Water Board, the 47 collieries along the river had stopped discharging mine wastes to the river;[237,238]
- The Sanitary Water Board had issued orders to 30 Schuylkill River municipalities and 500 industries to build or improve waste treatment by January 1st, 1951;[239]
- Three desilting pools had been constructed to catch coal wastes;
- Over 50 percent of the estimated 24 million cubic yards of culm had been removed from the river between Kernsville and Norristown;[240]
- Pennsylvania had committed funds to support dredging operations to finish the culm removal; and
- Lands for access to the river and for impounding basins associated with dredging at Plymouth and Flat Rock Dam were acquired.

The Schuylkill River Project Engineers reported that the project came in under budget[241] and was completed within the four years allowed by their contract with the Water and Power Resources Board. The total cost of the official Schuylkill River Project was $31,784,744.11 (approximately $300 million in 2012 dollars).[242]

All that remained was for Congress to appropriate the promised $12 million that had been estimated as the cost of the federal portion of the cleanup. But Congress was slow to act and provided fewer funds than the 1945 estimates for the federal government's share of the work even though the Schuylkill River Project Engineers reported that high flows during the project had moved large amounts of culm from above Norristown to the area below the dam during the period of time the State's project was underway.

Dredging below Norristown did not begin until 1952 when Gahagan Construction Company was awarded the contract to dredge the pools formed by Plymouth and Black Rock Dams. In 1953, American Dredging Company received a contract for dredging the pool formed by Fairmount Dam. The cost of these two contracts was approximately $3.6 million[243] far from the $12 million that had been anticipated in 1945.

The Department of Forests and Waters was responsible for acquiring land for the federal government's share of the dredging and acquired land for impounding basins convenient to the Plymouth and Black Rock dam pools and nearly 859,000 cubic yards of silt was pumped into the associated impounding basins.

Finding land for the sediments associated with the Fairmount pool was more difficult. In the vicinity of Fairmount Dam, as with the developed area around Reading, no lands with sufficient open space were available for impounding basins with the capacity for the three million cubic yards of sediment that would be removed from this reach of the river.

Instead of pumping to a nearby impounding basin, a new technique was used to move the dredged sediment. Three dredges, two in the pool created by Fairmount Dam and one below the dam, shared one common 11-mile long pipeline—the world's longest dredging line at that time—with four booster stations helping to move the dredged sediment. The last booster station was the steam-powered dredge "Pennsylvania."[244]

The U.S. Army Corps of Engineers' first choice for where to pump the Fairmount pool sediments was a 168-acre marsh, still within the Philadelphia city limits, but located at the City's southernmost fringe.[245] The property, which belonged to Gulf Oil Corporation, was a remnant of the once vast freshwater tidal wetlands known as Tinicum Marsh. The announcement that the last piece of the Tinicum Marsh was destined to be filled with coal silt and sediments dredged from the Schuylkill River mobilized local conservationists who had already documented the importance of the site to migratory waterfowl as well as resident bird populations. Local birders like Quintin Kramer and Allston Jenkins and conservation organizations like Delaware Valley Ornithological Club and the Philadelphia Conservationists, Inc., (which would become the Natural Lands Trust) mobilized to preserve the Tinicum Marsh.[246,247] In response, Gulf Oil agreed to donate 145 acres of the marsh to the City of Philadelphia for a wildlife sanctuary.[248]

Tinicum Marsh would again be threatened with filling in 1969 in association with the construction of I-95, but again the conservationists would organize to protect Pennsylvania's last freshwater tidal marsh. The federal government would step in and preserve the site as part of the Tinicum National Environmental Center. In 1991, it would be renamed the John Heinz National Wildlife Refuge at Tinicum in honor of the senator who helped protect it from development in 1970.

Instead of filling Tinicum Marsh, sediments dredged from the Fairmount pool were pumped to the Philadelphia International Airport for use as fill.[249] Another location proposed for deposit of the dredged sediments was Philadelphia's Eastwick section. The Philadelphia Redevelopment Authority proposed to pump sediments into this low lying area and redevelop a new city with housing for 45,000 people on top of the old neighborhood.[250] Dredged sediments were used to fill low lying areas in Eastwick, but the planned city-within-a-city never came to be. Philadelphia Redevelopment Authority failed to take into account the opposition of existing residents who fought the redevelopment.[251] Some homes were built upon the dredged sediments; many of these buildings are prone to subsidence.[252] The Eastwick area remains a target for redevelopment today.

Pennsylvania's Schuylkill River Project came to an official end in 1951; the federal government ended its work on the project in 1954.

Back in 1945, the Schuylkill was barely a river, filled with coal wastes and used as an open sewer by every town and industry along its banks. By 1955, the collieries and washeries had been forced to stop carelessly discharging coal wastes. Over 20 million cubic yards of coal waste had been removed from the river. Industries and municipalities alike had been ordered to install treatment plants or stop discharging.

The Schuylkill cleanup was a joint government project, and it served as a model for work that could be done to reclaim polluted rivers.[253] Programs to clean up other rivers in Pennsylvania and across the country were underway even before the Schuylkill River

Project was completed.[254] Perhaps once the worst river, it deserves recognition for also being the first to be cleaned up.

As I have decided to accept a position with the United States Steel Corp. I respectfully tender my resignation as Chief-of-Party with the Schuylkill River Project Engineers. During the three and one-half years I have been employed by the Project, my association has been such a happy one that I regret to sever connection with it.

I wish to thank all those concerned for their kindness and consideration shown me. I consider it a privilege to have been part of the association and its valuable work.

— R.L. Rosendale, 1951[255]

Working on the Schuylkill River Project

At its peak, the Schuylkill River Project employed 120 people directly, but taking into consideration the 23 contractors and 25 subcontractors,[256] the number of people employed in connection with the Schuylkill River Project was probably much higher. At the project's start, one source estimated the number could grow to well over 3,600.[257]

Surveying

One of the first tasks of the Schuylkill River Project was to re-establish the traverse of the river from the U.S. Army Corps of Engineers' survey conducted a decade before, from 1935 to 1937, to determine the volume of culm in the river. During their earlier survey, the Army Corps had established markers and monuments along the Schuylkill from headwaters to mouth. From these control points, they had sounded the river to measure levels of coal sediment on the river bottom. The Schuylkill River Project had to find markers placed over 10 years before, replace them if necessary, and then sound the river to determine the volume of sediment in the river once again.

Like the Works Progress Administration cleanup proposed in the 1930s, the Schuylkill River Project was also intended to be a jobs program to provide employment for those who had served during World War II, men like Richard L. Rosendale and his friend Willard J. Rafetto. Rosendale, now of Reading, had served as a Marine fighter pilot; Rafetto had served in the Army.

In an interview on June 20th, 2012, Rosendale remember how he heard, through his wife Helen, about the possibility of work with the Schuylkill River Project. The Rosendales lived in Pottstown at the time, and Helen Rosendale was employed as Executive Secretary to Edmund J. Fitzmaurice, a civil engineer with Day and Zimmerman. Fitzmaurice had been added to the staff of the Schuylkill River Project Engineers in the role of Construction Manager. So the recently discharged Rosendale and Rafetto went to Fitzmaurice to inquire about work.

With their engineering backgrounds—Rosendale had attended

Wyomissing Polytechnic Institute and Rafetto had gone to Villanova—the two men were just what the Schuylkill River Project needed and they were soon among its first employees. The Schuylkill River Project began its survey work in 1946 with three teams, or survey corps. Two additional survey corps were added later.[258,259]

Rosendale and Rafetto were each hired as a Chief of Party, Rosendale for Survey Corps #6 assigned to work in the Reading area and above, Rafetto for Survey Corps #1 assigned to the Oaks reach of the river. Equipment issued to the teams included tripods, transits, levels and chains as well as items such as machetes, axes, a whetstone, a sledge hammer, waders and a snake bite kit.[260]

In five and six man teams, the survey corps traveled the watershed from headwaters to mouth, in all types of weather. One of Rosendale's notebooks shows his team sounding coal silt in November and December 1948. Rosendale remembers working in weather so cold that it was hard to record soundings with a soft "H" pencil. He related how he and his team had gotten to know the men who worked on the nearby railroad. In the cold weather, they would stop the shifter[261] to ask for a five-gallon bucket of coals to warm their hands while they were working.

From the onset of their work, there were delays and complications. "It took forever to get access to the Engineers' maps," reflected Rosendale. He later added, "Their stakes had washed away or corroded. Some of the brass monuments remained but most of those were gone too." Cold weather and high flows would also complicate their work. Some landowners refused access. Rosendale recalls one landowner greeting them with a shotgun. Rosendale and his team opted to avoid confrontation and come back later. He later learned that the farmer had lost a leg in an accident that resulted when a piece of farm equipment encountered a monument left from the earlier survey done by the U.S. Army Corps of Engineers.

The first task for the Survey Corps was to chart elevations. The work of taking depth soundings of the river came next. To determine the amount of coal silt in the river, the length of the river was broken into ranges. Range lines were run at 90° angles across the river at roughly 100-foot intervals.[262] A cable would be run across the river to mark the range line. At approximately 10-foot intervals along the cable, the depth of water and depth of coal silt were sounded, or measured. The depth of coal silt was measured by pushing a probe into the sediments until it encountered resistance or a hard bottom. Survey teams waded in the river or used a small Jon boat to take these measurements. Rosendale describes the Schuylkill of that time as "mud...black with culm." He added, "I was always a fisherman. I used to catch fish from the river that were black with culm."

The work of the Survey Corps didn't end after the initial survey of coal silt was completed. Throughout the dredging, the Survey Corps had to be on hand to sound coal silt in ranges of 50 or 100 feet immediately before and immediately after the dredging work was done. This was to determine the amount of coal silt in the range and to confirm the amount removed by the dredging contractor who was paid by the cubic yard of sediment dredged. Rosendale recalls his team working overtime on Fridays to complete the post-dredging soundings. "If it rained, the range just dredged could fill in behind him [the dredger]." Heavy rains and high waters might move silt downstream into a reach just dredged. If this occurred, the contractor wouldn't get paid for the full amount he had actually dredged.

Because of Rosendale's tenure with the Schuylkill River Project, he was in a rare position to see all aspects of the work being undertaken to clean up the river. Before the end of the project, he was promoted to Assistant Engineer which allowed him greater opportunities to gain a perspective on the cleanup. He even had the opportunity to fly over the Schuylkill in a helicopter to observe where coal silt and other types of pollution were being discharged to the river.

Dredging

Rosendale recalled that Eastern Engineering and American Dredging Company brought in their own people to operate the dredges on the Schuylkill during the cleanup. But dredging continued for years after the official Schuylkill River Project was completed in 1951. Robert Williams, Tamaqua, was a dredge operator for a total of 39 years, first as an employee of dredging contractors beginning in 1959 and later for the State of Pennsylvania.

In a June 16th, 2012, interview, Williams recalled dredge operations running from spring to fall. During the Schuylkill River Project, dredging operations extended throughout the year, with work continuing as far into the winter as December and January in 1949[263] and February in 1951.[264]

For the most part, weather didn't deter dredging operations. "If it rained, they gave you a raincoat," said Williams. But high flows and flood conditions could bring dredging to a halt.

Dredging operations during the project, as well as during Williams' time, ran on three eight-hour shifts around the clock. "Dredges aren't made to sit," added Williams. Start-up of dredging operations can take as much as an hour. With contractors being paid by the yard, minimizing any time the boat wasn't dredging was considered essential.

Dredges on the Schuylkill River operated with crews of as many as eight men during the Schuylkill River Project and as few as four during the later years Williams worked on dredging the Schuylkill. The typical six-man crew that worked the dredges designed for the Schuylkill River Project would have a leverman, a first mate, two deckhands, an engineer, and an oiler.

"The leverman was essentially the captain of the boat," said Williams. The leverman was responsible for raising and lowering the cutterhead, operating the suction pumps, and changing the position of the dredge. Williams stressed that operating the dredge arm and cutterhead was an important skill. "Finding the proper depth was all done by feel, by sound of the motor, and looking at the vacuum and pressure gauges. There was no sonar," added Williams.

The first mate was responsible for adding or removing pipes from the line through which dredged sediment was pumped into impounding basins. He was also responsible for operating a small boat that would be used on occasions to maneuver the dredge.

The dredges did not have any propulsion mechanism. Cables connected the dredge to shore and, by winching in or letting out these cables, the dredge could swing from bank to bank. Forward movement utilized special poles called spuds which were attached to a frame on the back of the dredge. A spud would be lowered and the pole planted firmly in the riverbed allowing the dredge to pivot and swing forward. Spuds were raised and lowered alternately to "walk" the dredge forward.

The deckhands were responsible for the heavy lifting. The engineer serviced the engine and made repairs as necessary. The oiler was responsible for keeping the machinery lubricated, but during dredging operations, "everyone had to work as a team," stressed Williams.

Working on a dredge was physically demanding. "Everyone ended up with back problems sooner or later. It was hard work," said Williams.

Because the noise of dredging operations was so loud, crews communicated by sign language. "Even the electric dredges were noisy. They had a high pitched whirring noise," recalled Williams who himself has hearing loss from working on the dredges. In the 1950s, Schuylkill River Project communications, from the dredge to support crews on shore, utilized a mobile radio system, call letters KA2333.[265]

The use of mobile radio for the purpose of public safety dates to the 1920s. By 1939, the extent of mobile radio use for forest fire prevention prompted the Federal Communications Commission to establish and regulate Forestry-Conservation Radio as a separate classification within the Public Radio Services category.[266] By 1948, all of the Department of Forests and Waters' 150 fire towers and District Forester offices had access to radio communications.[267] It is unclear whether the Schuylkill River Project's 1952 license was issued under the Forestry-Conservation classification, but it is clear that the Project was an early adopter of a new and useful technology that experienced significant post-war expansion in Pennsylvania and across the country. The Federal Communications Commission did not establish the Local Government Radio Service classification until 1958.[268]

To remove the coal silt from the river, the cutterhead on the dredge arm would be lowered toward the riverbed. As the cutterhead spun into the sediment, hydraulic systems would suck in a slurry of water, coal silt, and river sediments. This slurry was pumped through a pipeline on pontoons to the shore and ultimately to an impounding basin. More water than coal silt, the Schuylkill River Project Engineers estimated that the slurry was approximately 15 percent solids.[269] In the impounding basins, the silt would settle out of the water which was allowed to drain back into the river.

Sometimes the cutterhead encountered submerged debris in the river such as tires, crumbled fenders, railroad ties, battered buckets, other junk, and at least one sunken canal boat.[270] During his June 20th, 2012, interview, Richard L. Rosendale recalled that sometimes dredge crews encountered Native American eel weirs made of logs anchored in the river.[271] The force of the impact could break the cutterheads. "Welders were busy all the time to keep them going," added Rosendale.

After their long service to cleaning up the Schuylkill River, the dredges "Berks," "Montgomery," "Schuylkill," and "Tamaqua" were all sold for scrap in the early 1980s lamented Williams in his June 16th interview. "Their engines were leaking PCBs," he said in explanation. The dredge "Chester," which was used on the Fairmount pool, was auctioned off after her service and acquired by the American Dredging Company.[272]

In the mid-1980s, a short time after scrapping the Schuylkill River Project dredges, Pennsylvania purchased a new dredge, one that could be operated by just four men, to remove the coal silt that continued to settle out in the desilting basins.

Pipelines

During his June 16th interview, Robert Williams recalled pumping dredged sediment up to one-and-one-half miles away. The Schuylkill River Project used boosters to move dredged sediment distances of nearly four miles.[273] The U.S. Army Corps of Engineers moved dredged sediment as much as 11 miles.[274]

The Water and Power Resource Board acquired access to a 40 foot strip along both banks of the Schuylkill for much of its length in part for the Schuylkill River Project Engineers to re-establish the survey and take soundings of the river, but also for running the cables that provided the electricity powering the dredges, and for running pipes from the dredges to the impounding basins.

The dredging contractors were responsible for assembling the pipelines that transported dredge sediments. Richard L. Rosendale remembered these companies tended to bring in their own people for the jobs, but occasionally they hired workers in the areas where they were dredging.

Daniel E. Ludwig, Pottstown, was recently married when his employer, Sanders and Thomas, ran out of work for him. In an interview on June 6th, 2012, Ludwig recalled looking for another job and seeing an ad in a local paper for work assembling pipelines for the dredges cleaning up the Schuylkill River.

He answered the ad and was hired for a bull gang, one of the crews of laborers tasked with assembling pipe to move the coal silt dredged from the river to the impounding basins along the Schuylkill's banks. American Dredging Company was looking for men to lay a line from the Black Rock Dam to the Oaks impounding basin, a distance of roughly two miles.

Ludwig worked on a crew of six men laying ten-foot sections of pipe. Two men would take a break while the other four men worked so the crew could keep a steady pace. They had over 1,000 pieces of pipe to connect for just this line.

The pipes had one narrow end and one flared end. The narrow end of one pipe was inserted into the flared end of another pipe. Then four men would use a ram against the pipe to force it to seat securely. Although shims were used to get a tight fit when there were leaking joints, no other fasteners were used to secure the pipe. With the force of the coal silt slurry being pushed through the pipe by the dredge, a tight fit was essential to prevent a blowout.

Checking the joints in the pipeline sometimes meant getting wet. During that cold fall of 1950, Ludwig's wife, Nancy, who joined Ludwig for his June 6th interview, remembers her husband coming home from work with icicles on his eyebrows. After just a few weeks, Sanders and Thomas had some work for Ludwig again and he returned to his job as a structural draftsman.

For those living near the pipelines, the sound of the 24-hour a day operations could be annoying. George Heckman, Hamburg, who grew up near the site of the Kernsville Dam, during his June 22nd, 2012, interview, remembered hearing the clang of stones, perhaps larger pieces of coal, rattling along in the pipelines on the way to the impounding basin.

Robert Adams, Hamburg, also grew up near the Kernsville Dam. He also recalled the dredges operating around the clock and the eerie feeling he would get going out along the walkway along the pontoons in the dark to see the dredge in operation at night.

Dams and Desilting Pools

The most obvious features on the landscape today that serve as reminders of the Schuylkill River Project are the Kernsville and Auburn dams, the Tamaqua weir, and the desilting pools created by these structures. Their construction was one of the benchmarks that needed to be completed to secure federal participation in the cleanup below Norristown.

Kernsville was the first dam to be constructed. In a June 22nd interview, Chester "Chet" Epting, Hamburg, recalled a project supervisor, who came to oversee the dam's construction, staying with his family during that time. Although Epting doesn't recall the man's name, he recalled that the man had come from Tennessee which suggests it may have been Joel B. Justin of Justin and Courtney and the Schuylkill River Project Engineers. Justin had worked with the Tennessee Valley Authority prior to the Schuylkill River Project. The Epting home, just one-half mile from the site of the dam, would certainly have been convenient for Justin.

The principal contractor for the Kernsville Dam was Poirier and McLane Corporation which was based in New York; however,

Poirier and McLane hired local workers, like Chet Epting and his brother Richard, and they worked with at least one subcontractor, Hamilton Construction Company, which leased some equipment locally.

Epting recalls pouring a lot of concrete that was mixed for the dam. In all, 70,000 cubic yards were used. The contractor set up its own concrete plant nearby and pushed an intense construction pace—nearly 200 men worked two eight-hour shifts daily[275]—to complete the project three months ahead of schedule.[276]

But that haste may have resulted in waste, or at least dissatisfaction with the contractor in the community. Clifford Mowrer of Spring City first took Hamilton Construction Company and then Poirier and McLane to court for damages to a tractor used during dam construction.[277] The case ultimately went to the Pennsylvania Supreme Court which reversed a lower court decision that had awarded damages to Mowrer.[278]

In a June 22nd interview, Robert Adams, Hamburg, recalled that property was taken from his father's farm for the dam construction. But when the contractor wrapped up operations, Adams' father found damages to his land that was adjacent to that land which had been taken for the project.

In his June 16th interview, Robert Williams, who would later work on the dredges, recalled that the acquisition of land—which included some taking by condemnation—for construction of the dams, desilting pools, and impounding basins, was not always looked on favorably. "A lot of farms up here lost a lot of acreage for not a lot of money," said Williams.

The community around the Tamaqua desilting pool had reason to dislike the Schuylkill River Project which essentially constructed the project right in the middle of a small town. "After dredging was done and the coal silt dried out, if the wind came up, you had to turn on your headlights to get through town," recalled Williams.

But the Schuylkill River Project was moving forward finally and nothing would stop it, not even the deaths of two staff members of the Schuylkill River Project Engineers. Tragedy struck during the construction of Auburn Dam, when a handbrake failed on a concrete mixing truck. Emil E. Larson, Principal Engineer, and James Daniel Byrne, Project Inspector, were observing concrete being poured for the dam when they were struck and killed by the runaway vehicle.[279]

Men of the Schuylkill River Project

Few remain with us today who can recall how polluted the river was before the Schuylkill River Project. Fewer still can give first-hand accounts of their part in the unprecedented project to clean up the river.

Although his time connected to the project was short, Daniel E. Ludwig feels good that he had even a small part in the cleanup. "People don't realize how bad it was," said Ludwig interviewed on June 6th, 2012. "You would never have fish in this river if it hadn't been cleaned up."

Growing up in the Pottstown area, Ludwig was very familiar with how polluted the Schuylkill was. His family's drinking water, provided by the Borough water authority, came from the river. Ludwig recalled the strong chlorine smell that came with the strong chemical treatment, "Everyone would get spring water to drink. We were one of the poorest families around and we went to get spring water to drink which shows you how bad it was." As late as 1947, the Borough of Pottstown was investigating damming the Manatawny Creek for its water supply.[280]

Even years later, the treatment of the Schuylkill still disturbs Richard L. Rosendale, interviewed on June 20th, 2012. "What they were doing was illegal," declared Rosendale. "The Schuylkill never had any importance to people who lived on it. Everyone was dumping in it. It should have been one of the nicest resources in this region of the state," he added.

Robert Williams has seen the river change a great deal in his lifetime. "Most people don't remember what the Schuylkill was like. It was choked off," he said during his June 16th interview. "It has trout in it now. It only had coal dirt and sewage before."

The Schuylkill is a river again thanks in part to the efforts of

Ludwig, Rosendale, Williams, and the many others who worked on the Schuylkill River Project.

More than two million tons annually of silt, which for more than a century was diverted to those waterways, is no longer entering the streams. This is the greatest accomplishment of its kind ever to be attained anywhere.

— Secretary of Health Dr. Norris W. Vaux, 1949[281]

Selling Silt

When the Schuylkill River Desilting Act was passed in 1945, the Schuylkill River Project was supposed to earn back some of the funds that were spent on it through the sale of the coal dredged from the river. But long before any river coal was available to be sold, the price tag for the landmark project grew beyond the proposed costs.

In 1945, a $5 million appropriation was made available to fund the program with a commitment to provide $5 million in the 1947 biennial budget. From the onset, it was projected an additional $5 million appropriation would be needed to pay for the cleanup. But in 1949, Governor Duff asked for an additional $25 million to finish the job. The first $5 million of that was an emergency appropriation signed in January to keep the project from running out of money.

The 1949 request was $20 million more than had been anticipated at the passage of the 1945 legislation, but even with the higher price tag, the appropriation was approved (with $17 million coming from the general fund and the remaining $8 million from Pennsylvania's General State Authority[282]) for a total project cost of $35 million in state funds.[283]

But 1949 also brought about a change in the beneficiary of the sale of any dredged coal. As a result of Act 305 of 1949, any income from the sale of coal silt would be deposited in the general fund instead of supporting the continuing costs of the cleanup, perhaps as a result of the increased price tag for the project.

Even before the launch of the dredge "Queen" in September 1948, the Schuylkill River Project Engineers were reporting that private interests were inquiring about buying the sediments to be dredged from the river.[284] At that time, they estimated that the purchase price might be as much as $1.00 a ton. At that price, the sale of the sediments removed from the river during the official Schuylkill River Project would have resulted in an income of nearly $18 million, well over half the project's final cost.

With the demand that had existed for river coal, it was not unrealistic for the Department of Forests and Waters to expect to sell the dredged sediments. River coal operations had been active on the Schuylkill as late as November 1947.[285] Winter weather would regularly put a halt to the reclamation of river coal, but in 1948 the industry was put out of business along most of the Schuylkill River in preparation for the river cleanup.

The ending of the river coal operations meant higher prices for some end-users, particularly those who employed heating systems suited to burning the smaller sizes of coal, such as industry and institutions. In 1948, the City of Reading was paying $4.90 a ton for Buckwheat No. 3, or Barley-sized river coal for use at its Maiden Creek pumping station and filtration plant.[286] With no river coal available in 1949, the City would have to purchase coal from the mines. At that time, Buckwheat No. 3 sized coal was being advertised for sale at $7.75 a ton,[287] which would mean a cost increase of over 50 percent.

In all, over 20 million cubic yards of sediment were removed from the river during the state and federal phases of the Schuylkill River Project. The weight of these spoils was estimated to be more than 10 million tons.[288] It was likely that the impounding basins contained marketable coal. As the official Schuylkill River Project drew to a close, the time had come to determine what to do with these sediments.

The dredged sediments needed to be analyzed first for content and BTUs (the measure of heat available upon combustion), before any sale could move forward. In February 1948, before the project began, the Department of Forests and Waters estimated the dredged sediments would be 50 percent coal.[289] By November 1948, the estimate had increased to 70 percent.[290]

But if the dredged sediments could not be sold, the Schuylkill River Project Engineers would have simply created a new environmental problem by moving the sediments from the river to the impounding basins along the banks. Previously, coal silt that was deposited by high water on farmlands along the river made those lands unsuitable for farming.[291] In 1961, a former river coal processing operation was given as the cause of reduced property values and the justification for a lower assessment.[292]

Even before decisions were made about the disposition of the dredged sediments, the fines were already being eyed for other purposes. In 1948, river sand and coal fines from a river coal operation were tested for spreading on icy roads as a replacement for the cinders normally used when supplies of cinders ran out.[293] It was also suggested that the state might use the coal wastes to heat its own facilities equipped to burn coal fines in order to reduce its own heating costs.[294]

In 1949, at least 90,000 cubic yards of silt, sand, and stone taken from the river were provided without charge to the Borough of West Reading.[295] The sediment was made available to the Borough by the contractor to fill in a low lying area along the Wyomissing Creek.[296] Whether this was with the permission of the Schuylkill River Project Engineers or the Department of Forests and Waters is unclear.

The Department of Forests and Waters may have hoped to sell the dredged sediments for as much as $1.00 per ton when it first opened the bidding on the material in four impounding basins above Reading in 1951. It was disappointed. Not one bid on the sediments was received.[297]

Later that year, the Department of Forests and Waters again advertised the material in the four impounding basins above Reading—Stoudt's Ferry, Eplers, Leisz, and Riverside—for sale. Two bids were received, but it was unlikely that either pleased the Department. For the rights to reclaim coal fines, sand and other materials from the 3.3 million cubic yards of dredged sediment in the four basins, the Locust Valley Coal Company bid $0.31 a ton; Charles D. Manbeck bid $0.18 a ton.[298] At the time, it was estimated that coal comprised 60 percent of the dredged sediments in the basins.

Manbeck, Schuylkill Haven, had operated river coal dredging operations as well as washeries along the Schuylkill and Little Schuylkill. He had even developed equipment to improve the ability to clean coal fines.[299] Manbeck, who was selling fines to power plants equipped to burn them,[300] likely had a good grasp of the effort that would be involved in cleaning the dredged coal silt, but Manbeck lost out to Locust Valley Coal Company.

Herman Yudacufski, Frackville, was the president of Locust

Valley. Unlike Manbeck, Yudacufski did not have experience with river coal (S. Cotler, personal communication, 3 July 2012). Other coal operations may have questioned his business decision, but Yudacufski must have believed he could make a profit even at the price he bid.

Before it could be used even by facilities equipped to burn fines, the coal in the basins needed to be cleaned and processed. Locust Valley Coal Company constructed a facility a few miles above Reading to clean the coal and to separate it from the sand, stones, and other materials that had been dredged out along with the coal.[301] The company was named the Stoudt's Ferry Preparation Company for that first facility located near an impounding basin on Stoudt's Ferry Road in Leesport.

The Stoudt's Ferry Preparation Company would be the only company to ever reclaim coal from the sediments dredged from the Schuylkill during the Schuylkill River Project. Moreover, other than the lone bid by Manbeck in 1951, no other company has ever bid for the rights to reclaim coal from the impounding basins (S. Cotler, personal communication, 3 July 2012).

Under its first contract, the Department of Forests and Waters was paid $0.31 a ton for the dredged sediments as well as $100 per month for use of each of four basins for a limited length of time.[302] The Stoudt's Ferry Coal Preparation Company began with three employees and operated one eight-hour shift.[303] The operation would grow to include operations in multiple locations along the river associated with impounding basin locations.

Stoudt's Ferry's contracts would be renewed over the years with some changes in the price to be paid for the reclaimed coal. By 1965, the price had increased to $0.35 a ton.[304]

When the Schuylkill River Project Engineers submitted their final report, they believed the project would need to continue for roughly five to eight years in order to remove the coal already in the river as well as coal wastes that would continue to wash out of culm banks.

From 1952 to 1962, an additional 1.3 million cubic yards of sediment was dredged out of the Kernsville desilting pool. The

Auburn desilting pool produced 3.35 million cubic yards of sediment in dredging undertaken from 1952 to 1963. From 1952 to 1964, an additional 1.3 million cubic yards of sediments came out of the Tamaqua desilting pool.[305]

But dredging didn't end as the Schuylkill River Project Engineers had predicted. Dredging continued beyond 1964 and was undertaken not just in the desilting pools, but along the length of the river at times. An additional six million cubic yards of sediments were dredged from the river between 1964 and 1985.[306]

Stoudt's Ferry continues to mine the sediments dredged from the river today. Operations are currently active near Auburn, Mount Penn, and Oaks; however, the company never found the dredged sediments to have the percentage of coal that the Department of Forests and Waters had estimated. During the early years, the amount of coal recovered probably ran no higher than 40 percent (S. Cotler, personal communication, 5 July 2012).

As technology has improved, Stoudt's Ferry's ability to extract coal from the sediments has improved resulting in repeated reclamation operations at various impounding basins. The operation near Mount Penn is currently extracting marketable coal at a recovery rate of approximately 18 percent from the refuse of its earlier reclamation undertaken back in the 1960s and 1970s (S. Cotler, personal communication, 5 July 2012).

Recently, the company received the contract to reclaim coal sediments from the Linfield Basin property located along the Schuylkill River in East Coventry Township, Chester County. The County now owns the basin. This was not the first effort to reclaim this basin's sediments. Still, Stoudt's Ferry removed 18,890 tons of coal silt for which they paid Chester County $18,890. Nearly sixty years later, the sediments are finally selling at the $1.00 a ton the Department of Forests and Waters had hoped for in 1951.

Even though the reclamation of coal continues today, the life of the business is limited. "We see an end to it," said Steve Cotler, current president of Stout's Ferry. "But as new processes evolve, we are able to remove more material. And the more we remove, the more viable the use of the land is after we finish," he added.

Many of the lands acquired by the Department of Forests and Waters for the impounding basins have been turned over to county and township governments. As Stout's Ferry completes its reclamation work, some of these lands have found new life as parks and open space areas.

The taking of lands for impounding basins had been criticized by some as simply a re-shuffling of the river's burden of coal silt. Indeed, tons of dredged sediments were stockpiled on these previously unaffected lands, but the impounding basins served an important and, in some cases, long-term role in the river clean-up. With the stored coal reclaimed, the successful restoration of these sites for recreational use stands as tribute to those who believed the Schuylkill clean-up was possible. These lands are part of the continuing legacy of the Schuylkill River Project.

1970 photo showing an abandoned coal cleaning plant and culm bank near Buck Run, Pennsylvania, in the Schuylkill River's headwaters. U.S. Bureau of Mines.

1973 photo showing an abandoned coal breaker and culm bank near Mary D, Pennsylvania, in the Schuylkill River's headwaters. U.S. Bureau of Mines.

A mountain of culm remaining from mining operations. The location of this culm bank, which was typical of many found throughout the anthracite region, is unknown. Enlargement from a 1970s-era photo. U.S. Bureau of Mines.

A sediment-laden Schuylkill, from an image that was included in The Schuylkill River Project: Restoring a Natural Resource to the People of Pennsylvania, *a 1948 publication by the Department of Forests and Waters to promote the Schuylkill River Project. Used with Permission of the Commonwealth of Pennsylvania, Department of Environmental Protection.*

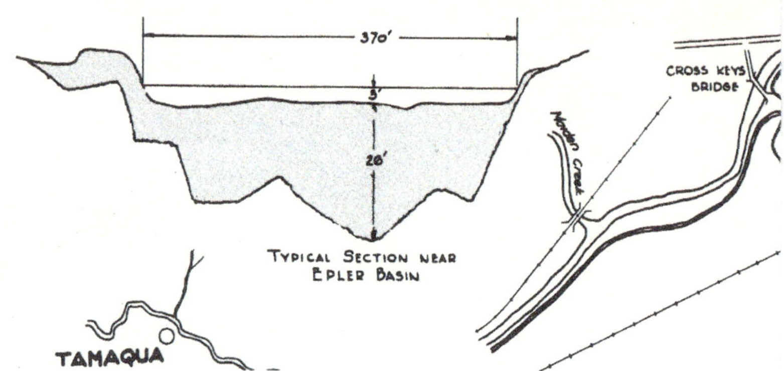

Cross-section of the Schuylkill River with the width of the river (370 feet) indicated as well as the depth of water (3 feet) and the depth of silt (26 feet). This detail was taken from a project map included in The Schuylkill River Project: Restoring a Natural Resource to the People of Pennsylvania by the Commonwealth of Pennsylvania, Used with permission of the Commonwealth of Pennsylvania, Department of Environmental Protection.

Dam removal near the Schuylkill River Gap. The removal of five dams was undertaken to allow silt to move further downriver where it could be removed. This image was included in The Schuylkill River Project: Restoring a Natural Resource to the People of Pennsylvania by the Commonwealth of Pennsylvania, Used with permission of the Commonwealth of Pennsylvania, Department of Environmental Protection.

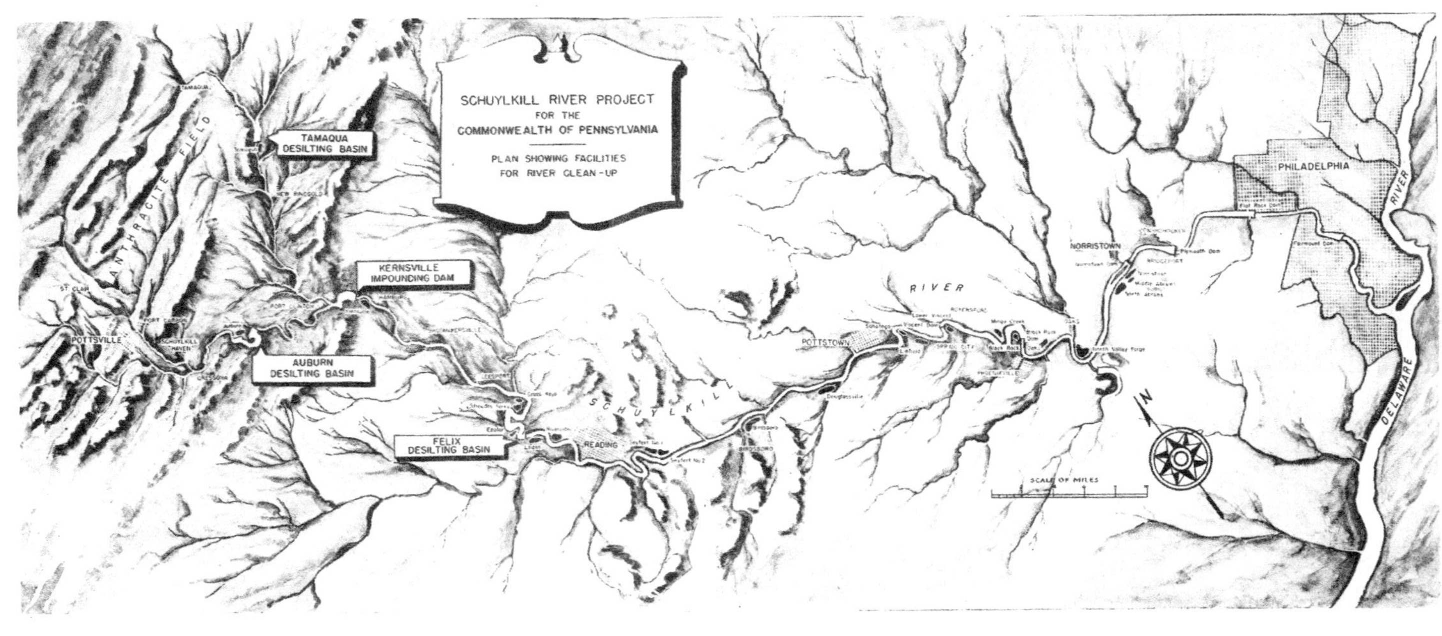

Map of the Schuylkill River watershed, included in the <u>*Final Report of the Schuylkill River Project Engineers*</u>*, indicating the locations of the facilities constructed for the Schuylkill River Project. Used with Permission of the Commonwealth of Pennsylvania, Department of Environmental Protection.*

Duff family group taken from a photo of the extended family gathered for Thanksgiving in 1899. Future governor James H. Duff (standing at right) is shown with his parents, Margaret Morgan Duff and Reverend Joseph Miller Duff. Courtesy of Robert Phillips.

Governor Duff (right) with John M. Phillips in 1948 at a ceremony to dedicate a historical marker commemorating the first purchase of state game lands, in 1920, made possible by the proceeds of hunting license fees. Pennsylvania Federation of Sportsmen's Clubs.

Governor Duff (center) with Phillips (at Duff's left) and Ross Leffler, Pennsylvania Game Commission (at Duff's right), at the 1948 ceremony commemorating the first purchase of state game lands. George Rupprecht. Courtesy of Russ Braun.

SCHUYLKILL RIVER PROJECT ENGINEERS
April 3, 1950

Disposition of Forces - Construction Div.

#10 - Henry D. Johnson, Jr., Asst. Construction Mgr.

#141 - E.E. Larson, Principal Engr. (Killed 2 June '50) - #17 - H.C. Hadley, Asst. Engr.

#25 - T. A. Trafford - Chief Inspector

Badge No.	Inspectors	Contract Assignment	Duty Station
62	W. P. Hall	Core Borings	Oaks
103	N. H. Magee	#30	Oaks
110	W. K. Thrush	#31	Pottstown
134	J. D. Byrne (Killed 2 June)	#35	Hamburg
135	J. J. Gillen	#11 & #34	Shoemakersville
155	L. T. Riis	#'s 10-R, 36 & 36-B	Hamburg
163	E. B. Boyle	Spring City Warehouse	Spring City
173	J. D. Pond	#24	Riverside
174	F. Costa	#25	Royersford

SURVEY CORPS

Classi-fication	CORPS #1 (Oaks - C-30)	CORPS #2 (Royersford)	CORPS #4 (Hamburg)	CORPS #6 (Riverside)	CORPS #7 (Riverside)
CH	38-W.J. Rafetto	63-W.A. Reese	48-J.L. Jones	85-R.L. Rosendale	72-P.F. Devere
⊼	37-G.H. Finnie	178-J.M. Korkus	161-G.W. Yoder	158-E.O. Long, Jr.	164-D. Geiger
ø	54-J.C.Monaghan	197-W.Z. Bowe	23-N.J. Simon	137-W.W. Miller	138-M.E.Kressly
ø	167-J.J. Uhrin	199-C.J.Thum, Jr.	166-F.O'Donnell	150-D.L. Ogden	49-C.G.Messick
ø	198-J.R. Denick		169-J.J.Anthony	159-J. Machette	165-D.G.Torok, Jr
ø	200-F.S.Massino			179-~~E.A. Bears~~ Bomberger	
Assignment	C-#'s 30 & 32	C-#25	C-#'s 10-R, 35, 36 and 36-B	C-#'s 11 & 31	C-#'s 24 & 34

HDJ:BMM
cc: E.J. Fitzmaurice
D.J. Walker
H.D. Johnson, Jr.
W.A. Black-C.G.Rodgers, Jr.
T.A. Trafford
H.C. Hadley
Corps #1
Corps #2
Corps #4
Corps #6
Corps #7

1950 document listing the names of those working in the Schuylkill River Project's Construction Division, which included the Survey Corps. Rosendale Papers. In possession of the author, Bristol, Pennsylvania.

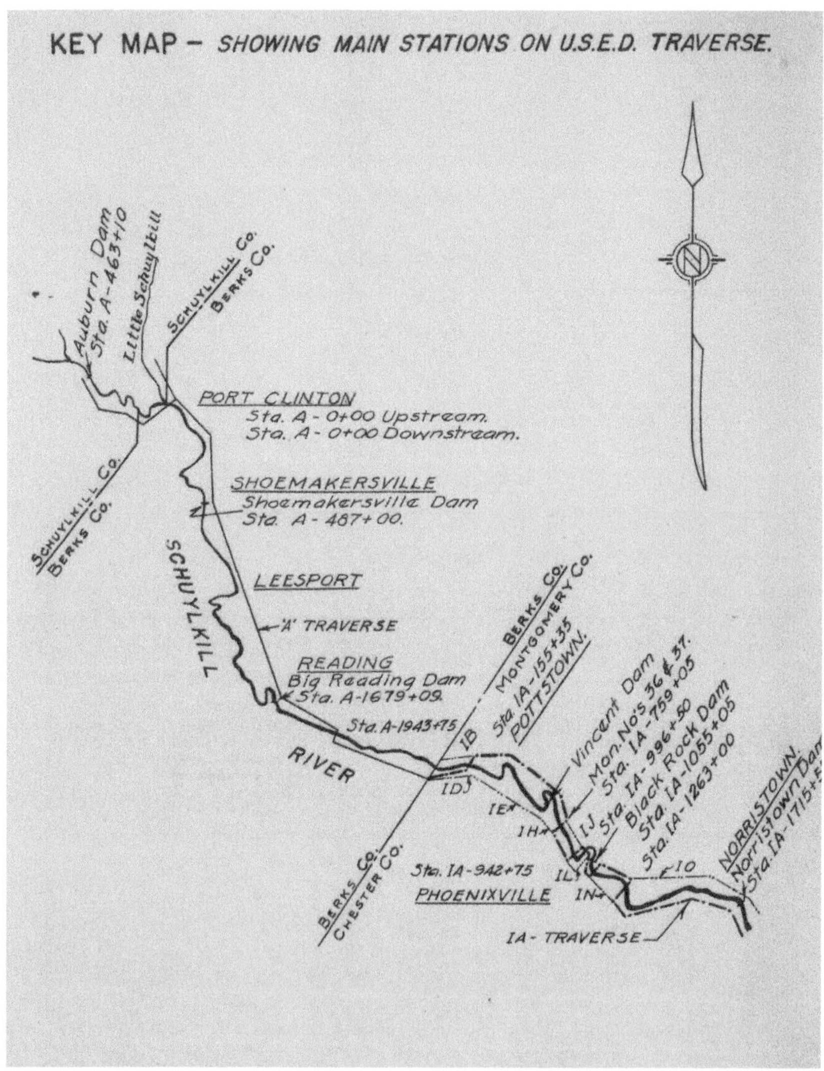

The Schuylkill River Project Engineers' map of the traverse stations from the U.S. Army Corps of Engineers' 1935 to 1937 survey. Re-establishing the traverse was among the first tasks undertaken for the Schuylkill River Project. Rosendale Papers. In possession of the author, Bristol, Pennsylvania.

Top right page 105: Field Notes from Survey Corps #6 showing range lines established at 90° angle to the river. Once established, range lines can be used for monitoring changes in the river over time. Rosendale Papers. In possession of the author, Bristol, Pennsylvania.

Bottom right page 105: Field Notes from Survey Corps #6 showing soundings of Range 2123. At intervals, from left bank to right bank, the depth of sediment was sounded across the range line and recorded. Rosendale Papers. In possession of the author, Bristol, Pennsylvania.

2

FELIX POOL

Layout of Ranges

Range	Traverse Sta	F.S.	Angle-R	Ref Hub L Bank	Ref Hub R Bank
R 2184	37+53	$35+50^{42}$	87°00'	+30' R	+406L Paint Mark on Cliff
R 2183	38+59	$37+59^{26}$	107°-30'	+62' L	+430 L
R 2182	39+53	$39+33^{12}$	108°-00'	+19' R	+280' L

A.J.P
1-5-49

2

Rosendale C.P. Corps VI
Long ⊼
Miller
Edgar
Machetto

Book 181

Dec 1 1948
Clear - Cool

POL $38+66^{12}$
Range 2184
Hub +30' R
87°00'
Flat +42' L
Flow
Flat +386' L
+406' L
Mark Painted on Rock Cliff
Rock Cliff

PI $37+59^{26}$
Range 2183
Hub +62' L
Flat +80' L
ISLAND
Flow
Flat +362' L
Hub +430' L

POL $39+33^{12}$
Range 2182
Hub +19' R
108°00'
Flat +20' L
Flow
Flat +228' L
Flat +260 L
Hub +280 L

A.J.P
1-5-49

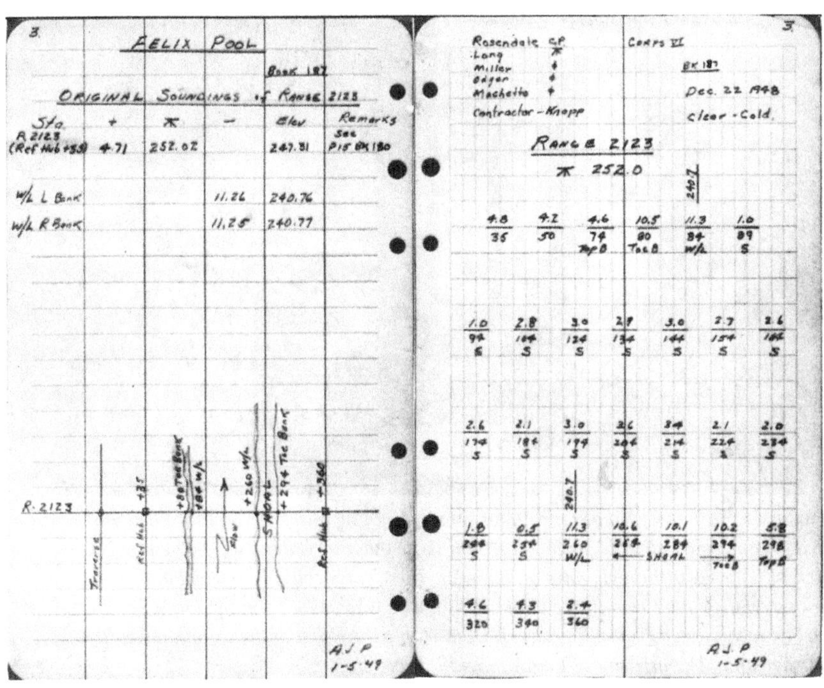

3.

FELIX POOL

Book 187

ORIGINAL SOUNDINGS of RANGE 2123

Sta.	+	⊼	−	Elev	Remarks
R 2123 (Ref Hub +35)	4.71	252.02		247.31	See P15 BK 180
W/L L Bank			11.26	240.76	
W/L R Bank			11.25	240.77	

A.J.P
1-5-49

3

Rosendale C.P. Corps VI
Long ⊼
Miller
Edgar
Machetto
Contractor - Knapp

BK 187

Dec. 22 1948
Clear - Cold

RANGE 2123

⊼ 252.0

240.7

4.8 / 35	4.2 / 50	4.6 / 74 Top B	10.5 / 80 Toe B	11.3 / 84 W/L	1.0 / 89 S

1.0 / 94 S	2.8 / 104 S	3.0 / 124 S	2.9 / 134 S	3.0 / 144 S	2.7 / 154 S	2.6 / 164 S
2.6 / 174 S	2.1 / 184 S	3.0 / 194 S	2.6 / 204 S	3.4 / 214 S	2.1 / 224 S	2.0 / 234 S
1.8 / 244 S	0.5 / 254 S	11.3 / 260 W/L	10.6 / 264	10.1 / 284	10.2 / 294 Toe B	5.8 / 298 Top B

← SHOAL →

240.7

4.6 / 320	4.3 / 340	2.4 / 360

A.J.P
1-5-49

Earth-moving to prepare basins to receive coal sediments. Harold Amster. Used with permission of the Spring Ford Area Historical Society.

Concrete weir that served as a drain for an impounding basin. As a basin filled with dredged materials, silt and sediment would settle out, but water was allowed to drain back into the river through gates on the weir. These gates could be opened and closed by pulling on the cables seen in the photo. This image was included in the Final Report of the Schuylkill River Project Engineers. Used with permission of the Commonwealth of Pennsylvania, Department of Environmental Protection.

Work on the berm surrounding an impounding basin. The outlet for the impounding basin effluent can be seen at lower right. Harold Amster. Used with permission of the Spring Ford Area Historical Society.

Grading of the top of an impounding basin berm. The impounding basin impact on the river's floodplain can be seen here. The river can be seen through the trees at top right. Harold Amster. Used with permission of the Spring Ford Area Historical Society.

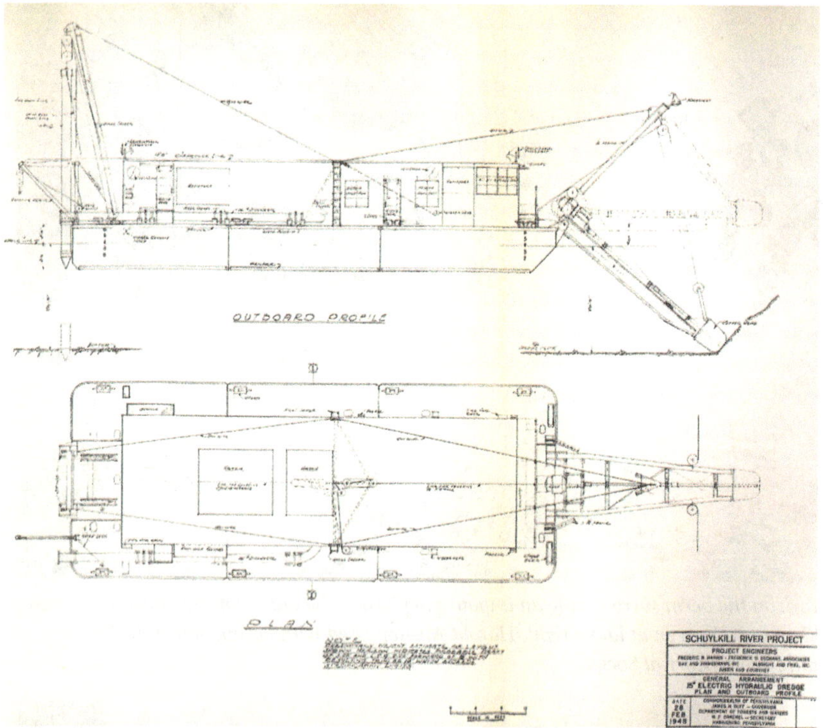

Design for four identical dredges constructed for the Schuylkill River Project. This drawing was included in the <u>Final Report of the Schuylkill River Project Engineers</u>. Used with permission of the Commonwealth of Pennsylvania, Department of Environmental Protection.

Top right page 109: 1949 launch of the Commonwealth Dredge "Schuylkill" at Parkerford, Pennsylvania. This image was included in the <u>Final Report of the Schuylkill River Project Engineers</u>. Used with permission of the Commonwealth of Pennsylvania, Department of Environmental Protection.

Bottom right page 109: Dredge in operation near the Phoenixville Railroad Bridge. A cable can be seen at left running to the dredge. By winching in the cable, which would be anchored to a point on shore, or letting the cable out, the dredge would work back and forth across the river. Harold Amster. Used with permission of the Spring Ford Area Historical Society.

Leverman operating a dredge on the Schuylkill. Harold Amster. Used with permission of the Spring Ford Area Historical Society.

The "Schuylkill" pumping into the Sanatoga Basin in 1949. This image was included in the Final Report of the Schuylkill River Project Engineers. Used with permission of the Commonwealth of Pennsylvania, Department of Environmental Protection.

Sediments that had accumulated in the floodplain were bulldozed into the river so the dredges could move them into the impounding basins. Harold Amster. Used with permission of the Spring Ford Area Historical Society.

The vegetation bulldozed into the river along with the floodplain coal wastes could clog the cutterhead, intake pipe, or pumps. Other debris in the river that could damage the cutterhead included tires, car fenders, railroad ties, and battered buckets. Harold Amster. Used with permission of the Spring Ford Area Historical Society.

8 a.m. 6/22/50 to 8 a.m. 6/23/50

Eastern Engineering Company

Sample

4 N. North Carolina Avenue
Atlantic City, New Jersey

DREDGE REPORT

Dredge Queen Contract No. 31
Date 6/23/50 Weather Good
Location Birdsboro Pool
Booster Pumps: Electric none Diesel X
Pipe Line 325' Engines Oper. 3
Right Bank Sta. R-3260 to R-3262
Center Cut Sta. R-3261 to R-3262
Left Bank Sta. R-3261
Yds. This Period 5,111 est yds/mo 184,429
Calculated Yds. as of

EFFECTIVE TIME Est. Yds./Hr. 258
Pumping hours this period 19 Hrs. 50 Min.

NON-EFFECTIVE TIME
Handling Pipe Line 45 Min.
Handling Swinging Lines
Change Location
Clear Pump and Stone Box 1 Hr. 25 Min.
Clear Suction 1 Hr. 15 Min.
Clear Pipe Line
Minor Repairs 45 Min.
Miscellaneous
Other
Lay Time Off
Lost Time
TOTAL Non Effective Time 4 Hrs. 10 Min.

Remarks: Shore Pipe @ R-3256+50 Rt. Bk.
Pumping into Birdsboro Basin.
R. P. M. 900 Pressure 50#

Prepared by R.N. Davenport

Dredge operations report detailing Eastern Engineering's dredging operations near Birdsboro, Pennsylvania, for the 24-hour period from 8:00 a.m., June 22nd, to 8:00 a.m., June 23rd, 1950. Rosendale Papers. In possession of the author, Bristol, Pennsylvania.

Construction of Linfield temporary dam in 1949. Temporary dams were used to impound water to make it possible for the dredges to operate. This image was included in the Final Report of the Schuylkill River Project Engineers. Used with Permission of the Commonwealth of Pennsylvania, Department of Environmental Protection.

Clearing coal sediments from the Schuylkill's banks near Reading. This image was included in the Final Report of the Schuylkill River Project Engineers. Used with Permission of the Commonwealth of Pennsylvania, Department of Environmental Protection.

Dredging sediments that have been moved into the River. At lower right, it can be seen that the Schuylkill River is flowing higher than the level of its floodplain. Harold Amster. Used with permission of the Spring Ford Area Historical Society.

A dragline moved sediment from the river's banks into the channel. Harold Amster. Used with permission of the Spring Ford Area Historical Society.

Looking upstream from Chester County toward Black Rock Dam, pipelines run along the towpath of the Chester County Canal, also called the Phoenix Branch Canal. Donald Kucharik. Used with permission.

A slurry of water, coal, and sediment is pumped into an impounding basin. The Schuylkill River Project Engineers estimated that the slurry was approximately 15 percent solids. Harold Amster. Used with permission of the Spring Ford Area Historical Society.

Dredged materials being discharged into the Stoudt's Ferry impounding basin. The Schuylkill River Project Engineers estimated that the slurry was approximately 15 percent solids. This image was included in the <u>Final Report of the Schuylkill River Project Engineers</u>*. Used with Permission of the Commonwealth of Pennsylvania, Department of Environmental Protection.*

The site of the future Kernsville Dam. This image was included in the Final Report of the Schuylkill River Project Engineers. Used with permission of the Commonwealth of Pennsylvania, Department of Environmental Protection.

Kernsville Dam under construction. This image was included in the Final Report of the Schuylkill River Project Engineers. Used with permission of the Commonwealth of Pennsylvania, Department of Environmental Protection.

Kernsville Dam under construction. Harold Amster. Used with permission of the Spring Ford Area Historical Society.

Top right page 119: The Tamaqua Desilting Basin was created by excavating eight feet below the level of the adjacent river bed. The Little Schuylkill was then diverted into the excavated basin, and its original channel filled. About 300 feet below the basin's outlet, where it returned to its channel, a weir was constructed across the river. This image was included in the Final Report of the Schuylkill River Project Engineers. Used with permission of the Commonwealth of Pennsylvania, Department of Environmental Protection.

Bottom right page 119: Water flowing over the weir at the Tamaqua Desilting Basin. This image was included in the Final Report of the Schuylkill River Project Engineers. Used with permission of the Commonwealth of Pennsylvania, Department of Environmental Protection.

Kernsville Dam, 2005 photo. Gregg Adams. Used with permission.

2005 photo showing stowage warehouse and dredge docking area, left, at Kernsville Dam. Gregg Adams. Used with permission.

2003 photo showing Stoudt's Ferry Preparation Company reclaiming coal from the Lower Vincent impounding basin. The double deck mobile screen unit, seen at right, separates material into three sizes. Used with permission of the Stoudt's Ferry Preparation Company.

2004 photo showing Stoudt's Ferry Preparation Company excavating dredged sediments from the North Abrams impounding basin to reclaim marketable coal. Used with permission of the Stoudt's Ferry Preparation Company.

At left: Ruth Patrick in the field. In 1948, Patrick led the teams that studied the Conestoga Creek, a tributary of the Susquehanna River, and pioneered the use of biological indicators for assessing stream health. © Academy of Natural Sciences, ANSP Library & Archives Coll. 2012-004.

Below: 1948 Academy of Natural Sciences' River Survey Crew. From left: John Wallace algologist; Thomas Dolan, IV, entomologist; Ruth Patrick, founder of the Academy's Limnology Department; Chuck Wurtz, invertebrate zoologist; Jackson Ward, chemist; and John Cairns, Jr., protozoologist. © Academy of Natural Sciences, ANSP Library & Archives Coll. 2012-020.

2006 aerial view of Black Rock Sanctuary wetlands, seen at lower right. An interpretive trail loops around the wetlands. Black Rock Dam and Lock 60 can be seen in the center of the photo. Christian Devol. Used with permission.

2012 photo showing a rain garden in the parking lot of Black Rock Sanctuary. Sustainable stormwater best management practices were incorporated into the development of the Black Rock Sanctuary. John Mikowychok. Used with permission.

2011 photo showing Union Township's two-mile handicap accessible loop trail, which circles the former Birdsboro impounding basin. The Township's trail connects to the Schuylkill River trail. John Salaneck, III. Used with permission.

2011 photo showing trail head amenities associated with the basin loop trail including a lighted parking area, a picnic pavilion, pedestrian bridges over the Schuylkill Navigation Canal, and a boat ramp. John Salaneck, III. Used with permission.

Kernsville Dam Recreation Area. 2005 photo showing the Schuylkill River near Pulpit Rock. Gregg Adams. Used with permission.

Kernsville Dam Recreation Area. 2008 photo of the trail and butterfly gardens in the area of the former impounding basin. Gregg Adams. Used with permission.

Looking downstream from Montgomery County toward the Linfield truss bridge, a meandering Schuylkill River flows in a channel filled with sediment. Enlargement from a 1949 or 1950 photo by Harold Amster. Used with permission of the Spring Ford Area Historical Society.

Looking downstream from mid-channel toward the Linfield truss bridge, 2012. C. Towne.

Kayaking on the Schuylkill River near Pottstown, Pennsylvania. 2004 photo. Ted Danforth. Used with permission.

This measure, which uses largely the organisms that are attached to the bottom or edges of the stream, will reflect the water conditions that flowed by a given point for a considerable time before sampling, whereas a chemical analysis can only tell us the condition at the exact time it was taken.

— Ruth Patrick, 1949[307]

Canaries of the Stream

For decades, miners really did take canaries into coal mines with them to serve as early warning systems for air quality. Carbon monoxide, which can be found in deep mines, is colorless, odorless, and potentially deadly. Carbon monoxide detectors are used today to alert miners to the presence of the gas, but in the past, canaries, and sometimes mice, served as biological indicators of air quality. If these small animals showed signs of carbon monoxide poisoning, the miners knew conditions were unsafe.[308] As recently as 1986, canaries were still being used in mines in England.[309]

Biological indicators—the aquatic organisms that spend all or part of their lives in the water—are also used to tell us about stream health. The presence, or absence, of more sensitive aquatic organisms tells us a great deal about the stream being studied.

Some of the foundational studies demonstrating the suitability of aquatic organisms as indicators of stream health were conducted in Pennsylvania in association with the effort to clean up the Schuylkill River.

> In the spring of 1948 the Sanitary Water Board of the Commonwealth of Pennsylvania asked the Academy of Natural Sciences of Philadelphia to conduct a biological survey of the streams of the Conestoga Basin. The purpose of this survey was to see if the organisms living in a stream could serve as indicators of stream conditions particularly as related to sanitary and industrial wastes.[310]

The Limnologist in Charge of this research project was Dr. Ruth Patrick, an early advocate for the use of biological indicators.

In 1948, Patrick was head of the Limnology Department at the Academy of Natural Sciences of Philadelphia, but Patrick had begun her association with the Academy in 1933 as an unpaid researcher. The Limnology Department that Patrick founded would later be named the Patrick Center for Environmental Research in her honor. Among the many recognitions bestowed upon Patrick during her long career—Patrick taught at the University of Pennsylvania for 35 years—was the Distinguished Daughter of Pennsylvania award in 1952 (this award program was established by Governor James Duff in 1948 and named its first honorees in 1949).[311] This award was in part in recognition of Patrick's role in the stream cleanup effort.

At the Academy, Patrick also helped pioneer multi-disciplinary studies and as a result was in a position to mentor many young scientists in the field of aquatic ecology. Among the young scientists working with Patrick on the studies of the Conestoga was John Cairns, Jr. Cairns, who received his Ph.D. from the University of Pennsylvania, would go on to work with Patrick at the Academy for a number of years, even serving as Acting Chairman of the Limnology Department for a year, before leaving to teach first at the University of Kansas and later at Virginia Polytechnic Institute.

Cairns wrote[312] about his participation in the 1948 study:

> My first experience working on a river survey research team was the 1948 Conestoga Creek Basin study with the Academy of Natural Sciences. The two teams formed by Dr. Ruth Patrick also studied the tributaries of Conestoga Creek, and my team had the pleasure of sampling Lititz Run below the waste discharge of the Suchard Chocolate factory— one of the best smelling waste discharges I encountered in my entire career. I had responsibility for a major component of the research project— protozoologist on one of the two teams (Mary Gojdics was the protozoologist on the other team). Financial support for the team's research came from the Commonwealth of Pennsylvania. The goal of the research was to study the effects of pollution on the entire community of aquatic organisms, plus the water chemistry of the Conestoga Creek Basin and, to a much lesser extent, Brandywine Creek. These systems were chosen because they had a range of conditions from healthy to polluted. The basic hypothesis was very simple— the biota of a stream integrated all chemical/physical information

over time and, therefore, was the best way to assess pollution. Furthermore, each regional ecosystem was part of the Biosphere that covers the entire planet.

History

Any environmental history must be viewed in the context of the particular era. As a child born in 1923 before the Great Depression, I witnessed the effects of pollution upon the Schuylkill River and also heard about the revegetation of previously forested land by the Civilian Conservation Corps. During World War II, I became well aware of society's debt to science and the respect the general public showed to scientists.

After World War II, the pent-up demand for automobiles, housing, and consumer goods required that the large factories operate constantly to turn out material goods. The increased point-source waste discharges from factories and sewage treatment plants still were usually not so potent that rivers and streams could not recover, at least partly before the next point-source discharge. Pesticide use was not as common as it became in the last half of the 20th century, so non-point sources of pollution, such as fertilizers and pesticides, had not yet become a major problem. However, concern for any additional polluted discharges led to the organization of the river survey teams from the Academy of Natural Sciences in Philadelphia.

Team Research vs. Lone Wolf Scientists

In the 1940s and 1950s, team research was viewed as the only option for scientists who could not "make it alone." Team research has long since proven its value in the study of complex systems, but vestiges of the old view still remain. Individual research remains essential for a variety of reasons, but the stigma once attached to team research is nearly gone. One of the many attractive features of team research is that individuals on teams can be replaced without interruption of the team's continuity if both the team and new member are willing, even enthusiastic. However, citizens must also develop a long-term relationship with the ecosystem near where they live, and new residents must be welcomed to join the riverkeepers or similar groups. The scientists and local citizens must also develop long-term working relationships. Naturally, a group of people who are neither fishing nor swimming attract attention, and scientists should be delighted to explain what is happening with their research.

Working on team research was a new experience for all the members, and Ruth Patrick had not headed a team before. So the ability to closely collaborate was crucial and had many advantages. For example, everyone had access to the data of other investigators and could observe each specialist working. Each person seined for fish as a group effort and exchanged samples of their collections of other taxonomic collections. I often used samples the algologists collected because they might, and often did, have a species or two that I had missed. Even when the samples did not show new species, I was reassured that the protozoan samples I collected were representative of that area. Since freshwater protozoa are both perishable and likely to multiply, I would leave the study area and return to the laboratory as soon as I had a representative set of samples (i.e., all common habitats). Since the team had 48 hours allotted to each sampling area, working steadily and systematically was important. Most field samples could be preserved for later study, but not protozoans.

Although the team members were strangers to each other, they all knew Ruth Patrick from previous experiences. She was responsible for the team spirit— which Ruth and I have still reminisced about in the 21st Century. We were not only a group of specialists— somehow we were two groups on a single team from day 1. Without that sense of community, the Conestoga Creek Basin study might have failed. An illustrative example of group harmony is that no one took a shower— symbolizing the end of the work day— until all members of the team had returned safely from the field.

Procedures

One goal of the Conestoga Creek Basin study was to determine how much sampling was enough. Each crew member collected specimens from each habitat in the sampling area until 30 minutes passed without finding a new species. I followed the same procedure with the individual samples I examined when I returned to the laboratory. This process ensured that the collections were representative but not redundant.

All team members worked long hours with no overtime. I often worked until midnight and sometimes until 2 a.m. Of course, we enjoyed our work, but the major factor was the freedom to publish the results both as a team and as individuals. The sponsor also benefited because publication in a peer-reviewed, scientific journal demonstrated the high quality of the research.

Even though 60 plus years have passed since the Conestoga Creek Basin study and the statistical methods, sampling methods, and chemical analyses have improved, the examination of the organisms inhabiting an ecosystem remains the most reliable

> indicator of ecosystem health and integrity. Similar studies carried out in many parts of the U.S., Canada, and the Amazon River now constitute valuable baseline evidence to document how much change has occurred since the baseline studies were initiated.

In addition to Patrick and Cairns, the scientists who participated in the 1948 study of the Conestoga included:

Algologists

John L. Blum, Professor of Botany, Cassin College

John H. Wallace, University of Pennsylvania

Bacteriologists

Donald Reihard, Jr., Pennsylvania State College

Raymond L. Smith, Pennsylvania State College

Entomologist

John W. H. Rehn, Cornell University

Invertebrate Zoologists

Thomas Dolan, IV, Cornell University

Herbert W. Levi, University of Wisconsin

Charles B. Wurtz, University of Pennsylvania

Protozoologists

Mary Gojdics, Professor of Zoology, Beret College

Vertebrate Zoologist

James A. Jones, University of Minnesota

Water Chemist

John M. Ward, Rutgers University

Chemical sampling can provide a snapshot of stream conditions reflecting only that moment in time when the water was collected, but, as the saying goes, a river is "never the same river twice." The biological indicators that Patrick, Cairns and the other member of the Conestoga study examined and used to establish measures of stream health serve to provide a more complete picture of overall stream conditions. These measures are still relied upon today.

At the time Patrick's teams undertook the study, assessment of stream health focused on measuring the amount of oxygen necessary to break down organic wastes and on the stream's buffering capacity, its ability to resist changes in pH.[313] At the time, the idea of looking at biological indicators was considered as a possible supplemental method to measure water quality. Since that time, however, biological monitoring has taken a central role in studies of stream health. Since the late 1980s, the U.S. Environmental Protection Agency has encouraged the expanded use of biological indicators for assessing stream health.[314]

Another member of Patrick's team was Thomas Dolan, IV. Dolan made a career as a consulting biologist, and he has had a species of mayfly, *Leptohyphes dolani*, named in his honor. A prominent conservationist, he helped found the Pennsylvania Chapter of The Nature Conservancy as well as Pennsylvania's Natural Heritage Program. He also helped to found the Pennsylvania Environmental Council.

Dolan recalled studying the river during the time of the Schuylkill River Project.

> The Limnology Department of the Academy of Natural Sciences of Philadelphia conducted a survey of the Schuylkill River. One of the goals of the study was to identify the impact of acid mine drainage upon the river. One of the survey stations was located in the vicinity of Leesport, north of Reading, in Berks County.
>
> As survey entomologist, I was searching for aquatic insect species. In spite of rigorous collecting efforts, I only found one adult beetle. The larval stage of the species is aquatic, but the adult does not qualify as an aquatic organism. Therefore, it was not included in the listings of aquatic organisms. I cannot recall if we collected any other macroinvertebrates at that station.
>
> The fact that no aquatic insects were found living at that location on the Schuylkill was indicative of the

> presence of acid mine drainage...The other pollutant of major significance in the rivers at that time was coal culm (silt). Silt clogged habitats in the river bottom, rendering them unavailable to many of the aquatic organism required as food for fish.[315]

Today, many volunteers across the country utilize monitoring protocols to assess stream health that are based on the work of Patrick and her teams. Data collected by these volunteers are used by watershed organizations to advocate for stronger protections for healthy streams and the cleanup of polluted streams.

"We're not just training volunteers to assess biological indicators. We are empowering citizen scientists with the capability to engage regulators and insist on the necessary protections for their local streams," said Faith Zerbe, Monitoring Director for the Delaware Riverkeeper Network which has had a volunteer monitoring program in place for over 20 years.

"Knowing that the protocols we use in stream monitoring today are based on landmark work done in Pennsylvania in the 1940s and 1950s provides important perspective for the work we do today," continued Zerbe. "It also means we have a responsibility to carry forward that legacy by doing our best to protect the freshwater we all need to survive and thrive."

In addition to the biological studies conducted on behalf of the Sanitary Water Board, the Department of Forests and Waters undertook investigations to measure stream flow and sediment concentrations as well as to study other physical characteristics of the Schuylkill River. These studies were a coordinated effort by the Department of Forests and Waters and the U.S. Geological Survey. Study objectives included:

- Demonstrating the effectiveness of the cleanup program and the procedures implemented by collieries and washeries to stop coal waste discharges;
- Documenting Pennsylvania's progress in meeting federal sediment removal benchmarks;
- Developing capability to measure effectiveness of the desilting

pools;

- Collecting data on soil erosion unrelated to coal mining;
- Gathering data on acid mine drainage; and
- Providing information on water quality to encourage industries to locate facilities in the Schuylkill River watershed.[316]

Eight sampling stations were established: Port Carbon, Landingville, Auburn, Drehersville, Berne, Pottstown, Graterford, and Philadelphia.[317]

Dredging of coal sediments began in September 1948, but some discharges of coal wastes continued until June 1949.[318] The changing nature of the Schuylkill sediment was observed during these studies:

> The most apparent characteristic of the suspended sediment in the Schuylkill River has been the black appearance owing to the coal. This has been one of the identifying characteristics of the Schuylkill River for many years. Only in the past few months have suspended-sediment samples, particularly from the lower stations, shown somewhat the appearance usually associated with sediment resulting from erosion of the natural soil mantle.[319]

Sediment discharges measured at Landingville and Berne in 1948 were found to be 30 to 40 times higher per square mile than sediment discharges outside of the mining regions.[320] The annual sediment discharge per square mile below the Auburn desilting pool dropped from 3,700 tons to 30 tons after the Schuylkill River Project. For the Little Schuylkill River at the Tamaqua weir, the annual sediment discharge per square mile dropped from 10,000 tons to 950.

The joint water resource investigations had shown that the Schuylkill's sediment load was reduced significantly by the Schuylkill River Project, but they also demonstrated that the project had no effect on the acid mine discharges. Unregulated acid water from the mines was continuing to flow into the Schuylkill and, unfortunately, would continue to do so for years to come.

It will cost the State money, it will cost industry money, it will cost mills and mines money, and it will cost municipalities money but it is money that must be spent and must be spent now because we face a problem that must be solved now. To defer action will cost a lot more money later and possibly it will then be too late.

— Attorney General James H. Duff, 1945[321]

The River Endures

For the Schuylkill, the river cleanup marked an important turning point. Without the Schuylkill River Project, the river's future as a water supply was debatable. Before the project, the Schuylkill's ability to function as a river was significantly compromised.

In 1947, the concept of river restoration was something new. The Schuylkill River Project Engineers themselves described the work they oversaw to clean up the Schuylkill as "restoration," but river restoration is an evolving science. Today, it is unlikely that those working in the field would consider the Schuylkill River Project to be a "restoration."

One modern definition of river restoration is "assisting the recovery of ecological integrity in a degraded watershed system by reestablishing natural hydrologic, geomorphic, and ecological processes, and replacing lost, damaged, or compromised biological elements."[322] The Schuylkill River Project Engineers were not looking to restore ecological integrity; they were endeavoring to restore the health of the Schuylkill River by freeing it of millions of tons of coal wastes.

The intention of the project was never to restore the Schuylkill to some pre-disturbance state. Governor Duff, the project's top advocate, wasn't even seeking restoration to a pre-coal mining era.

> [I]t should be made perfectly clear that in an industrial age like our own it is not physically possible to restore the streams to their pure and uncontaminated condition as they were when this state was agricultural rather than industrial as it now predominantly is.[323]

Duff's focus was water quality: "There are, however, definite standards of good water for an Industrial age and it is those good standards that our program should attempt to attain."[324]

For the Schuylkill River Project, improving water quality in the river simply meant getting the silt out. Even the language in the preamble to the Schuylkill River Desilting Act that blamed discharged coal waste for frequent flooding included among the consequences of flooding the spread of disease associated with the polluted flood waters as well as loss of life and property.

With water quality in mind, not river restoration, the Schuylkill River Desilting Act specifically authorized the Water and Power Resources Board to "correct the existing and prevent the future silting of the Schuylkill River and its tributaries by wastes from anthracite coal mining operations."[325]

The program pursued by the Schuylkill River Project Engineers on behalf of the Water and Power Resources Board focused primarily on the volume of sediment being carried by the river and the impact of that sediment volume on the capacity of the Schuylkill channel to move flood waters. Like any river, the Schuylkill, along its journey from headwaters to mouth, is always moving sediment, picking up particles in one reach and depositing them in the next.

Rivers seek a state of balance where the amount of sediment flowing in the river is no more and no less than the stream's carrying capacity. When sediment entering a river system is greater than the river's carrying capacity, when that sediment exceeds the stream's power to move it, sediment accumulates in the river's channel.

The volume of coal wastes and other sediment clogging the Schuylkill's channel was estimated by the Schuylkill River Project Engineers before they started work; they put that volume at 24 million cubic yards. Coal silt had accumulated in the river's channel, raising the elevation of the bed, filling the floodplain, decreasing the channel's capacity, and increasing the frequency of flows over topping the river banks. By 1945, for much of its length, the river was choked with black silt, more a coal slurry than a river.

It did not require a hydraulic engineer to recognize the harm that had been done to the Schuylkill by these sediments. Deposits of coal silt 26 feet deep and floodplains filled with culm were clear indicators that something was wrong with the river. For decades, a massive sediment load had been discharged to the river. It was widely described as "too thick to navigate, too thin to cultivate." Clearly, the Schuylkill's sediment load was exceeding the river's carrying capacity.

But perhaps more was going on here. River systems are complex with interconnected biological and physical processes. From Native American eel weirs, to the milldams on tributaries, to the Schuylkill Navigation dams and canal cuts, to an enormous cut and fill project that changed the river's course near the Schuylkill River Gap, the river had endured the effects of human impacts for centuries. But like dominoes, altering any one element in a river system brings about changes in another, each affecting river function.

Because the City of Philadelphia adopted the Schuylkill as its source of drinking water, the river has been the focus of ongoing study since the early 1800s. As concerns over water quality began to be voiced, worries about water quantity also were expressed. In 1885, the Philadelphia Water Department saw how clearing the Schuylkill watershed's forests had reduced the volume of water flowing in the river.[326]

The Philadelphia Water Department had documented a 50 percent decrease in the river's summer low-flows over a period of 60 years.[327] William Ludlow, Chief Engineer for the Philadelphia Water Department in 1885, recognized the connection between precipitation and the river's base flow, or the normal amount of water in a stream fed largely by groundwater. Moreover, he understood the connection between vegetation and the infiltration that replenishes a river's base flow. Ludlow also understood that the clearing of forests in the Schuylkill watershed—the conversion of forest to farms and towns—had affected the river's flow regime; i.e., the variations in its flow.[328]

Ludlow's observations on the reduction in the Schuylkill's lowest flows came at a time of significant growth in the coal industry. The Schuylkill's hydraulic load—the amount of water in the river system—was being diminished even as its sediment load was about to be dramatically increased with coal wastes.

Complicating this alteration of the Schuylkill's flow regime were the 32 dams associated with the Schuylkill Navigation system. These were run-of-the-river dams—the amount of water flowing over the dam is equal to the volume of water moving in the river, not water storage structures. These dams likely had little effect on flood flows,[329] but they may have worsened the effects of low flow conditions downstream.

The Schuylkill Navigation dams trapped sediment, catching first the soil washed from farm fields and development as the watershed was cleared of vegetation. Later, they would catch the culm discharged by collieries and washeries as mining expanded in the river's headwaters.

Patterns of sediment accumulation behind a dam may vary,[330] but the builders of the Schuylkill Navigation dams likely expected some sediment to accumulate in pools and canals. In 1836, 12 years after the official completion of the canal system, a steam dredge was purchased by the company.[331] By 1847, it was determined that deeper impoundments and canals were necessary, in part to accommodate a larger class of boats. Deeper pools were temporarily achieved by raising the height of the dams, but dredging was the proposed method to provide the deeper draft.[332] As of 1854, the company was having difficulty maintaining channels in the impoundments behind the uppermost dams due to coal wastes.[333]

When dams trap sediment in impoundments, they can make for a "hungry" river downstream. After a river has dropped out sediment behind a dam, it flows downstream scouring its bed, down-cutting its channel, and eroding its banks to pick up the sediment it needs to balance its hydraulic load. These conditions likely occurred along the Schuylkill during the operation of the canal system.

The Schuylkill's watershed had been deforested; the river was dammed, and its bed dredged. Even before massive amounts of coal wastes were discharged to it, the Schuylkill was deserving of a restoration. But what might be termed the first attempt at restoration of the Schuylkill was a limited project. In length, it encompassed the main stem from Auburn to Fairmount Dam, a much larger project than would usually be considered for a river restoration today. But in scope it attempted only to reduce the river's sediment load to what might more closely resemble natural conditions for the system.

The plan developed by the Schuylkill River Project Engineers to clean the river of its coal wastes began with selective dam removal to restore more natural river flows that would be better able to move sediments than the slackwater behind the dams was. This first step in the Schuylkill River Project might meet with approval from today's river restoration practitioners, but the dredging that followed is another story.

Dredging can be damaging to a river system. Dredging a stream and deepening its channel can alter stream flow patterns, velocity, and dynamics. Despite the best intentions, dredging can cause increased erosion and changed flooding patterns, causing flooding where before there was none, even make existing flooding worse. Gouging out the bottom of streams and removing river bed sediment and woody debris can harm important aquatic ecosystems by removing habitat and food sources.

Some modern river restoration projects like that being undertaken on the Kissimmee River in Florida incorporate limited dredging to restore meanders to the channelized river. More often, river restorations are undertaken today to attempt to undo the damages that resulted from dredging done in the past.

And even before the Schuylkill River Project's dredging phase got underway, the practice of dredging had a long-established history on the Schuylkill. It was dredged for canal traffic and for saleable river coal. Federal involvement in dredging the tidal reach began in the 1870s when the shallowest depth at low water was 16 feet.[334] Today, portions of the tidal Schuylkill are more than twice that depth at mean low water.

Whatever the extent of dredging, it did not keep pace with the volume of sediment, as much as two to three million tons of coal waste,[335] that made its way into the Schuylkill River every year for decades. Through 1963, the total volume of fine waste produced in the coal fields of the Schuylkill watershed has been estimated at 70 to 80 million tons and a significant portion of that waste made its way into the river.[336]

The river coal dredgers at most recovered a few hundred

thousand tons of coal each year.[337] The Schuylkill River Project brought dredging to the river on a massive scale. During the official project and the dredging that followed, it was estimated that at least 18 million tons of sediments were removed from the river.[338] But this leaves over 50 million tons of fine waste. Some of these wastes may be found in culm banks in the Schuylkill's headwaters. Some may have been burned to produce energy at a cogeneration plant. And some of them remain in the river.

But the material dredged from the river was not only coal wastes. The Schuylkill River Project Engineers estimated that as much as 70 percent of the dredged sediments were recoverable coal;[339] however, others did not believe the percentage of coal was so high. In 1944, in dredging undertaken prior to the Schuylkill River Project, as much as 50 percent of the dredged sediment was "valuable soil from our farms and hillsides."[340]

In the experience of the Stoudt's Ferry Preparation Company, the percentage of coal reclaimed from the dredged sediments may have reached as high as 40 percent, with 30 percent being the average (S. Cotler, personal communication, 5 July 2012). In the course of reclaiming from the impounding basins, the Stoudt's Ferry Preparation Company has found thousands of tons of slag waste from small steel mills as well as soles of shoes, toys, metal objects, and more (S. Cotler, personal communication, 7 July 2012).

Sounding the river bottom during the Schuylkill River Project to determine the volume of coal wastes accumulated there was not an easy task. Today, this work would be done using a precision depth sounder, a global positioning system, and hydrographic survey software. During the cleanup, the Survey Corps sounded the riverbed using a transit, levels, surveying tape, level rod, and range poles. Measurements were recorded with paper and pencil (R. Rosendale, personal communication, 20 June 2012).

During the soundings, the Survey Corps determined the depth of coal silt by pushing a probe into the sediments until it encountered resistance or a hard bottom. This was done before and after dredging, but a number of high flow events occurred during the dredging phase and not all Survey Corps were able to re-survey the sediments promptly after dredging (R. Rosendale, personal communication, 20 June 2012). Any delays between initial surveys, dredging and follow-up surveys might allow upstream sediments to move into an area changing the composition of materials before dredging or filling back in an area that was just dredged, which opens the possibility that the composition and volume of sediment dredged from the river could differ from the numbers reported by the Schuylkill River Project Engineers. There is also the potential for some variability in the accuracy of the Survey Corps which could affect the measure of total sediment dredged and the estimated composition of that sediment.

If the percentage of coal that was in the dredged sediments is lower than what was estimated by the Schuylkill River Project Engineers, it simply increases the likelihood that a significant amount of coal fines remain in the river. Credence is given to this belief by a study undertaken by the U.S. Geological Survey, Philadelphia Water Department and West Chester University in 2006. During this study, sediment cores were collected from the Black Rock and Fairmount Dam impoundments. Analysis of the cores found:

> widespread distribution of coal in the lower basin. Sediment descriptions and ESEM [environmental scanning electron microscopy] analysis of selected cores identified fine- to coarse-grained sands of crushed coal in horizons up to one meter thick.[341]

But the coal wastes in the river weren't the only concern of the Schuylkill River Project Engineers. The stream cleanup plan also included clearing the river's channel. Over the course of the Schuylkill River Project, this work was described as channel rectification and channel training. Channel rectification generally refers to straightening; channel training refers to efforts to restrict the river's horizontal movement. Like dredging, these practices can be damaging to a river ecosystem, and they are the very kind of past impacts that modern river restoration seeks to reverse.[342]

Channel rectification and channel training have long been undertaken for the purposes of navigation and flood control. Reducing flood frequency and flood heights may have been among the goals the Schuylkill River Project Engineers had in mind when these activities were undertaken along the Schuylkill, but they seem to have become more important as goals after the fact. The 1968 report, *Water Resources of the Schuylkill River Basin* (Biesecker, et al.), asserts that "The goal of this work [the Schuylkill River Project] was to restore original slope and geometry of the river's channel."[343] However, no such statement is included in the reports of the Schuylkill River Project Engineers. Although these documents list flood damages among the impacts resulting from the discharged coal wastes, the work done to reduce flooding does not have a high profile in project reports.

Whatever the impact of the dredging and channel clearing on flooding, justification of the river cleanup as a flood control project seems to have been put forward almost as an afterthought for a project under scrutiny.[344] The early goals expressed for channel training, like the dredging, focused on coal silt.

> 1. Channel training includes the removal of excess deposits of culm on the natural stream banks and the removal of brush and undergrowth to minimize further accumulations of silt in times of flood flows.
>
> 2. It also includes the provision of a defined channel for the passing of low flows, thus preventing their spreading into thin streams over the whole river bed. This is a means of insuring the carriage of eroded silt and storm water without nuisance to riparian owners....[345]

Of the $31 million spent to carry out the Schuylkill River Project, less than $400,000 was spent on all channel clearing work.[346] For accounting purposes, the Schuylkill River Project Engineers did have an accounting category for field work related to flood control, but this category had only two subcategories, Reading and Schuylkill Haven. And even then, it did not rise to the level of having an accounting code assigned to it.[347]

If the Schuylkill River Project Engineers did intend to reduce flooding, floods in 1948,[348] 1950,[349] 1952,[350] and 1955[351]—all occurring after dredging had begun—would seem to say their efforts failed. By 1955, the project was even being blamed for increasing flooding problems.

Engineers critical of the dredging point out that while the flood crest never equaled the record height, the river rose faster than ever before. They suggested that the culm in the streambed had retarded the water.[352]

Specific channel clearing work undertaken during the Schuylkill River Project included both the opening and closing of channels in the river, removing land between the river and the remaining canals, and changing the width of the river. Other in-stream work included removing sunken barges, old coal recovery equipment, and the bottom sills of old dams.

Certainly such debris could have contributed to localized flooding, but the channel clearing also included clearing the 40-foot strip right-of-way of "brush" and vegetation with trunks less than three inches in diameter (measured at a point 4-1/2 feet above the ground) as well as the removal of both tree stumps and overhanging trees. If indeed the Schuylkill River Project sought to reduce flooding and flood damages, we know now that this type of clearing may have only made flooding worse.

Today, we know that floodplains vegetated with trees and shrubs can be as much as four times more effective at slowing flood flows as grassed areas.[353] Moreover, healthy, vegetated floodplains provide benefits beyond absorbing flood flows. The floodplain's periodically inundated vegetation also helps to cleanse runoff and remove nutrients from floodwaters.[354]

Maya K. van Rossum is the Delaware Riverkeeper and leader of the Delaware Riverkeeper Network. Serving in this role since 1994, van Rossum has influenced state and regional policy and regulation in a wide array of water quality, quantity, and habitat matters including flooding, floodplain protection, stormwater runoff, water withdrawals, oil spills, and toxic and other pollution discharges. van Rossum laments the Schuylkill River Project Engineers' misguided efforts to enhance the Schuylkill's ability to pass flood waters by clearing vegetation from a 40-foot strip along both sides of the river.

> The Schuylkill River Project Engineers missed a great opportunity to increase protection for the river through the establishment of vegetated buffers. With streamside buffers, we know the wider the buffer the better. At a minimum, the Schuylkill River should have buffers 100 to 300 feet in width, but planting 40 foot buffers after the cleanup would have made a good start. The Department of Forest and Waters could have used the example of the Schuylkill to lead the way toward better buffer protection across Pennsylvania decades ago. Instead we are still fighting for better buffer protection today.

The plan undertaken by the Schuylkill River Project Engineers may have had another flaw as a flood control project. The impounding basins constructed to hold the dredged sediments occupied considerable land area in the river corridor. All told, the basins occupied nearly 1,500 acres. Many of these basins were in the floodplain. As a result of the impounding basin construction, the already flood-prone Schuylkill's active floodplain was narrowed, which would increase flooding and decrease stream stability elsewhere.

> Along the river in the northwest corner of the [Valley Forge National Historical P]ark the floodplain has been drastically altered by the construction of a large dike. This dike was constructed as part of a coal silt removal operation in the Schuylkill River. As a result, the active floodplain is very narrow in this area. The area behind the dike is severely altered due to deposition and subsequent removal of coal silt.[355]

Todd Moses, a Geomorphologist and Senior Restoration

Specialist for Skelly and Loy, has worked on the assessment of watershed and stream conditions and the design and construction of stream rehabilitation projects in Pennsylvania, Oregon, Washington, Idaho, Alaska, and California. Beginning with his work on the Boulder Creek project in Colorado in 1986, Moses has worked on stream rehabilitation projects for 26 years. Moses does see work done by the Schuylkill River Project as an attempt to address flooding in a developed landscape that allowed little room for the river to move:

> The massive Schuylkill River desilting and flood control project of the post-war 1940s was designed to clean accumulated sediment from the channel in order to alleviate future flooding. From a conservationist's standpoint, the modifications to the river were undoubtedly heavy-handed... although this intervention was undoubtedly brutal with respect to the normal functioning of riverine ecosystems and associated river processes and landforms, this or a similar project may well have been necessary in the heavily-settled landscape traversed by the Schuylkill River.[356]

The volume of coal silt deposited in the Schuylkill and its floodplain compromised the river's natural function. The Schuylkill River Project Engineers attempted to restore that function through a program of dam removal, dredging, and channel clearing. Today, we have the benefit of a deeper understand of how rivers function, but research conducted at facilities like the Patrick Center for Environmental Research at the Academy of Natural Sciences or the Stroud Water Research Center is adding to our understanding even now.

Restoration Specialist Todd Moses provided some additional perspective on the efforts of the Schuylkill River Project Engineers to restore the Schuylkill:

> Current stream and watershed restoration projects in Pennsylvania do not begin to approach the

> scale of this project [the Schuylkill River Project]. Yet this massive project—and the equally massive disruptions to the river's headwaters that precipitated it—underscore two major axioms relevant to environmental management and conservation in our time. These principles must now inform rationales for proposed ecologically beneficial interventions at all scales, from the removal of high dams obstructing fish migrations to localized stream corridor rehabilitation projects to native meadow restoration.
>
> The first axiom or precept is that we are now living in the Anthropocene Era, the geologic period during which human dominion has become pervasive over the entire Earth. This latest era, which commenced just a few hundred years ago, is evinced by a biosphere which has been profoundly altered and occupied by humans, is now substantially governed by human needs and desires, and continues to be altered by people at an ever-increasing rate. Future anthropogenic changes to the biosphere will carry us in directions which are fundamentally unpredictable. In terms of cause, effects and ultimate response, the historical situation on the Schuylkill River provides an exquisite illustration of the awesome power of humans in the Anthropocene Era.
>
> The second necessary precept is that the biophysical functioning of the planet has always been fundamentally driven by change. Ecological and geomorphic conditions in the Schuylkill River watershed were different when the first European settlers arrived than they had been only a relatively few thousands of years earlier. Conditions today, several hundred years after the European invasion, are vastly different still.[357]

In hindsight, preventing coal silt from ever being discharged to the river would perhaps have been the simplest way to protect the

Schuylkill, an important lesson to consider as we are called on today to make resource management decisions for our rivers, systems that we increasingly understand are extremely complex and fragile. The life of a river is long, and it may take years or even decades to see the results of our impacts, which is all the more reason to be cautious in our decision-making.

The Schuylkill may have endured human efforts to "improve" the river for our benefit, but they were not borne meekly. From 1924 to 1926, the Reading Railroad Company worked to cut a new course for the river at the Schuylkill River Gap. During the course of the construction, it was reported that the hard stone, through which the new channel was being cut, wore down in days the teeth on the steam shovels that should have lasted for months.

The flood-prone Schuylkill didn't make the job any easier. "At one time a flood carried thousands of tons of silt into the new bed, burying machinery and causing a large loss to the company."[358]

Heavy rain, high waters, and harsh weather similarly plagued the Schuylkill River Project. Impounding basin construction was delayed by conditions too wet for earth moving.[359] During the dredging, heavy rains caused the river to rise so rapidly that a contractor working to remove coal silt from an island near Birdsboro lost heavy machinery to the Schuylkill's flood waters (R. Rosendale, personal communication, 20 June 2012). Flood flows at Kernsville carried a crane over the unfinished dam (G. Heckman, 22 June 2012).

The Reading Railroad Company and, to some degree, the Schuylkill River Project Engineers believed they knew best how to manage the river. But a river charts its own course; the Schuylkill has been teaching this lesson for years. The next generation of river stewards would be wise to keep it in mind.

The Schuylkill River is acid from the coal fields to the upper city limits of Reading. At a point approximately 7 miles above Reading, the Maidencreek, a large tributary draining a limestone region empties its alkaline waters into the acid Schuylkill. These waters mix at river bends, at rapids and passing over dams until they reach Shepp's Dam at the upper city limits of Reading. At this point the river water rises above pH 7.0 and the stream remains generally on the alkaline side until it joins the Delaware.

— Robert S. Chubb and Paul L. Merkel, 1946[360]

Acid to Reading

The river cleanup program was popular at the time it was undertaken, applauded as long overdue. That opinion was likely helped by the public relations efforts of Governor Duff and his administration. In 1946, the Department of Forests and Waters began publishing a bi-monthly magazine entitled *Pennsylvania Forests and Waters.*[361] When paper was available to do so, 7,000 copies of each issue were distributed free to public and school libraries. During Duff's term as governor, Pennsylvania's stream cleanup campaign and the Schuylkill River Project were featured.

The Sanitary Water Board had its own publication, *Clean Streams*, but it did the Department of Forests and Waters one better, spending $65,000 on a film showing the progress made to clean up the Schuylkill River.[362]

Despite these efforts there was criticism of the Schuylkill River Project, even before the dredging was completed. The first criticisms focused on the compliance of coal operations with the ban on the discharge of coal silt.[363] But the criticism would grow to include those directly involved with the project.

The Schuylkill cleanup, as well as Duff's other infrastructure upgrades, had not come cheaply. Governor John S. Fine, the man Duff had supported as his successor, allowed the unpopular one-cent tax on 12 ounces of soda to expire. But Fine needed to raise revenue to support his own funding priorities as well as the financial obligations his administration had inherited. Duff and the Schuylkill River Project were given some of the blame for Fine's budget battles.

Governor Duff had made enemies in politics among opposing Democrats as well as his own party. With Duff gone to Washington, D.C., to serve in the U.S. Senate, those enemies attacked Governor Fine, Forests and Waters Department Secretary Draemel, and the Schuylkill River Project.

Fine certainly had different priorities from Duff. In Fine's first budget, funding for the Department of Forests and Waters was cut by nearly $5 million;[364] however, he had promised during his campaign to continue Duff's stream cleanup work and, to that end, nominated Secretary Draemel to continue as head of the Department of Forests and Waters.

Draemel had been lauded for his role in the Schuylkill cleanup in October 1950. At the dedication of Kernsville Dam, he was the hero:

> "Citizens of Pennsylvania, and particularly of Reading, Philadelphia, Easton and other areas are under an eternal debt of gratitude to Admiral Draemel who has been in charge of the Department of Forests and Waters during this work," Duff said. "He has amazed even engineers in the rapidity and success of this enterprise."[365]

Just a few months later in 1951, he was under fire at confirmation hearings in the Senate. Draemel was accused of heavy-handed management of his department, patronage, and improper management of lands and money. As of March, Draemel was the only member of Fine's cabinet who had not been confirmed by the Senate.

Chief among Draemel's detractors was John H. Dent, a Democrat from Westmoreland and the minority leader. The Schuylkill River Project was the centerpiece of Duff's accomplishments as governor. By criticizing Draemel, Dent was criticizing Duff and the Schuylkill River Project.

> "One thing he [Draemel] did make positively clear," said Dent [after Draemel answered questions before a closed door session of the Senate Nominating Committee], "was that the money spent by Duff on the Schuylkill River has not improved the quality of the water one bit."[366]

A long-time Duff opponent, Dent was up for lieutenant governor on the Democratic ticket in the race that Duff overwhelmingly won to become governor. Dent then challenged Duff's administration on issues ranging from his cabinet nominees[367] to proposed taxes[368] to the cost of food along the Pennsylvania Turnpike.[369]

Draemel served the Fine administration throughout 1951 without a confirmation vote. In December, the Senate finally voted, but the 26-14 outcome fell nine votes short of the required two-thirds majority. Immediately after the Legislature adjourned, Fine reappointed Draemel as Secretary of Forests and Waters. Draemel, however, was tired of Harrisburg politics and resigned in January 1952.

Not yet done with attacks on the Schuylkill River Project, in 1955 Dent spurred the Pennsylvania Senate to launch an investigation into the sale of dredged sediments.[370]

Nor was Dent the only critic of the Schuylkill River Project. Paul E. Sanger, an auctioneer and one-time Lebanon County Commissioner, criticized the project as not only wasteful, but damaging to the environment.

> Look at the millions spent on his so-called stream pollution projects where many hundreds of river bottom farmlands were made useless for all time by being buried under silt, gravel and coal. I have seen what took place from the air over the Schuylkill and Susquehanna River Valleys. That money would come in very handy with the unemployment situation as it is today.[371]

Sanger had supported Robert Taft as the Republican candidate for president in 1952; Duff had supported Eisenhower. In 1956, Sanger challenged Duff for the U.S. Senate in the Republican primary; Duff won easily.

Political squabbling had succeeded in casting doubt on the value of the project. And now Duff and Draemel were both out of the picture and not in a position to provide any defense for it. What's more, the implementation of the cleanup was causing some of those who had advocated for it to think twice about its costs.

Dredging silt from the Schuylkill was only part of the cleanup effort. As the dredging was going on, the Sanitary Water Board was ordering municipalities and industries to build treatment plants for the sewage and industrial waste that had long been discharged to the river. Many of the facilities, especially those along the Schuylkill, had been given a deadline of January 1st, 1951, but it takes time to secure funds, make plans, and build or upgrade treatment plants. Some facilities needed extensions to complete the proposed construction or required plant upgrades.

In their efforts to comply with Sanitary Water Board orders, Dr. Russell E. Teague, Pennsylvania's Secretary of Health, reported that the Commonwealth was leading the way in waste treatment.

> Pennsylvania, Dr. Teague said, was one of the first states in the nation to tackle the pollution "on a comprehensive basis."
>
> The state, he said, "has literally been the workshop of the nation in developing methods and techniques of control. Most of the major procedures and steps that have been taken here were without precedent in the country."[372]

But this work did not come without a steep price. Near the close of 1952, Teague estimated that $200 million had been spent in that year alone by municipalities and industry to comply with the Sanitary Water Board's treatment orders with at least half of that spent on construction.[373]

In the upper Schuylkill River watershed, where there were no treatment facilities, Schuylkill Haven was the first municipality to begin construction after the Sanitary Water Board's order. The estimated cost was $760,000. The City of Philadelphia, which had long pushed for the coal waste cleanup, was spending $60 million.[374]

In 1951, the City of Reading was attempting to renovate its plant in compliance with the Sanitary Water Board's order to improve its treatment plant and expand capacity, but the City had not yet advertised for bids to renovate its plant when a new problem developed. On March 1st, a 30-inch cast iron pipe carrying sewage from the City to its Fritz Island treatment plant broke. For 67 days, until May 7th when the pipe was finally repaired, nine million gallons of raw sewage flowed into the river every day.[375]

The Schuylkill River Project was blamed for the broken pipe, put down to a blow from the heavy dredging equipment. However, dredging in this part of the river had been completed in November

1950, over three months before the breach.[376] Ironically, the broken cast iron pipe had been installed over 50 years before by William H. Dechant, father of Schuylkill River Project Engineer, Frederick Dechant. At the time it was installed, the pipe was supposed to be resting two feet below the level of the river bed.[377]

But the 800-pound gorilla in the Schuylkill River watershed was acid mine drainage. The Schuylkill River Project had done nothing to stop the acid waters flowing into the river. It had never been intended to. But Duff's administration had sought to present the Schuylkill River Project in the best light possible. The project's supporters had said little about the mine drainage problem.

Certainly hopes had been high for what would be accomplished by removing the river's immense burden of coal silt, but it is highly unlikely that Duff, Draemel, or anyone connected with the Schuylkill River Project Engineers thought that removing the silt alone would restore the river's health. And there are indications that those involved with the project were fully aware that mine drainage would continue to be a problem:

> McCawley [Deputy Secretary, Department of Forests and Waters Edmund S. McCawley] expressed his opinion that the Felix basin should become a haven for fish and other water life because it is fed by the waters from the Maiden Creek, which flows into the Schuylkill at Cross Keys. The limestone content of the Maiden Creek should neutralize any mine wastes in the Felix basin, McCawley said.[378]

The waters of the Schuylkill had once run black with coal silt; they now ran clear. This was heralded by project supporters as a mark of success. But people like Robert Adams, Hamburg, who were living along the river at the time, knew there were still problems. Adams recalled, "The water was clear. You could go swimming without getting covered in coal silt." But he also recalled, "The way your hair and skin felt when you came out, you knew something was wrong. It was the acid," added Adams.

Acid mine drainage had enjoyed exemption from legal challenge or regulation since *Pennsylvania Coal Company v. Sanderson* in 1886. In the 1870s, Philadelphia Board of Health chemist Dr. Charles Cresson had hailed the mine acid in the Schuylkill as offering protection from disease that might otherwise be contracted by drinking the river's water. Cresson's belief was not a radical one, and it was held by many for decades to come.

> Limited amounts of mine drainage improve the quality of the water to which it is mixed. Iron serves as a coagulant and clarifier; it also removes other impurities. The acid acts as a disinfectant, but since water containing large amount of mine drainage is hard, saline and acid, it is necessary, in order to fit it for drinking purpose, to neutralize, soften and filter it.[379]

This philosophy, was in part, behind the Sanitary Water Board's policy of not requiring sewage treatment of discharges already receiving acid mine drainage discharges.

But there were some who questioned the concept that mine drainage improved water quality. In 1945, Robert Scheifley Chubb was the Chief Engineer for the City of Reading. A native of Reading and a graduate of Pennsylvania State University, Chubb had previously served as City Water Engineer as well as Water Superintendent for the Borough of Hamburg.[380]

Chubb, who saw the effects of mine drainage on the Schuylkill first-hand, began to question the accepted wisdom. In 1945, he wrote Attorney General Duff about his theory:

> There is no question as to the reduction in number of organisms occurring when domestic sewage is discharged into a stream carrying acid waters, but there is no evidence to cause us to assume the acid is selective, reducing the number of pathogenic organisms and permitting the desirable ones to survive. As those desirable ones are necessary to cause biochemical decay, the acid water by killing them or inhibiting their activity, it preserves or

> pickles the organic load, rather than disposing of it.[381]

Chubb's research was published in the *Sewage Works Journal* the next year[382] and presented a powerful argument for the Sanitary Water Board to order sewage treatment even for streams that were also receiving acid mine drainage.

Just as it is difficult to comprehend the volume of coal waste discharged to the Schuylkill over decades, it is difficult to grasp the volume of acid mine drainage pumped into the river. In 1945 when Chubb first contacted Duff with his theory about the effects of mine drainage on sewage, it is estimated that roughly 20 billion gallons of acid water were pumped from the mines to the Schuylkill, based on the figure of 53 million gallons pumped per day that was derived from data provided by the U.S. Bureau of Mines, Pennsylvania Department of Mines and Mineral Industries, and various coal companies.[383]

The U.S. Geological Survey provides as an example for visualizing one million gallons a swimming pool "267 feet long (almost as long as a football field), 50 feet wide, and 10 feet deep."[384] Now picture 50 such swimming pools and you will have the volume of acid water pumped into the Schuylkill in 1945.

The Clean Streams Law of 1937 had exempted both coal silt and acid mine drainage from regulations, but only until solutions could be found to deal with these problems. In 1945, it was felt a solution had been finally found to deal with coal silt. Technology was available for collieries and washeries to trap culm and stop its discharge and so the Brunner Bill, the 1945 amendment to the Clean Streams Law, was passed to remove the exemption for coal wastes.

For most of the 1950s, the volume of acid mine drainage pumped to the Schuylkill would exceed 25 million gallons per day. Although the volume of the acid mine discharge was decreasing, pumping to the Schuylkill would continue until 1965 when acid mine drainage was finally brought under regulation.[385] Even in 1965, the volume of acid mine drainage pumped to the Schuylkill was nearly 16 million gallons per day. The acid waters pumped to the river represented 38 percent of the lowest average daily flows as measured at Berne that year.[386]

The program's detractors were not wrong when they declared the river was still polluted. Minority leader Dent was not entirely inaccurate when he said:

> "That whole Schuylkill program was sold to the legislature on the ground that it would clean up the river and provide those people with decent drinking water.
>
> "It is safe to speculate that there's more acid in the Schuylkill River right now than before the program started."[387]

But he was being disingenuous. Dent had served in the Pennsylvania Senate as Democratic Floor Leader when the Schuylkill River Desilting Act was passed in 1945. The Desilting Act was passed to make the Schuylkill River Project possible. The Act was often described simply as "appropriating funds to dredge silt from the Schuylkill River."[388] Or it was lumped in as part of the post-war construction spending.[389] Stopping mine drainage had, unfortunately, never been part of the plan.

Every man, woman and child of today
and tomorrow has and will have
ample cause to be grateful to those of
Pennsylvania's present administration who
are successfully fighting the clean streams
battle of this Commonwealth.

— Lower Merion Rod & Gun Club
member Ellen A. Dietrich, 1950[390]

Breaking with the Past

At its most basic level, the joint state and federal Schuylkill River Project accomplished the removal of several Schuylkill Navigation dams and approximately 20 million cubic yards of sediments from the river as well as the construction of three desilting pools. But with the benefit of time, it may be that what the Schuylkill River Project deserves recognition for is less what it accomplished and more what it represented: a break with the past and a change in the way Pennsylvania's rivers would be treated.

Post-war Pennsylvania was at an environmental crossroads. Other Pennsylvania rivers were contaminated by sewage, industrial wastes, acid mine waters, and culm, but the Schuylkill was the poster child for how polluted a river could become.

Communities that took their drinking water from the Schuylkill were seriously looking at other, cleaner sources of water to replace it. In Pottstown, tapping the Manatawny Creek was considered.[391] Philadelphia had long looked at streams in the Poconos to replace the polluted Schuylkill.

In 1945 and 1946, just before the cleanup was to officially get under way, the push for Philadelphia to find a new water supply was heightened when Philadelphia's mayor appointed a commission to study the most cost effective way for the City to have better drinking water.[392] This commission appointed a group of engineers to study the problem. The appointed engineers included future Schuylkill River Project Engineer Francs Friel of Albright and Friel and Joel D. Justin of Justin and Courtney, the father of Joel B. Justin who also served among the Schuylkill River Project Engineers.

A number of options to bring drinking water to Philadelphia were considered, including moving the City's intake farther upriver, damming a stream in the Poconos to create a reservoir, and bringing water from as far away as the Delaware River Water Gap. In an interesting twist, an opponent of the Delaware River Water Gap plan was the Lehigh Coal and Navigation Company,[393] one of the very companies that Philadelphia had been pursuing for decades to stop discharging coal wastes to the Schuylkill. The Lehigh Coal and Navigation Company proposed the City acquire land that the company owned along the upper Lehigh River. Water would be diverted from the Lehigh to the Schuylkill via the Perkiomen Creek and ultimately to Philadelphia.

But the Schuylkill was not abandoned as a source of drinking water. The Schuylkill River Desilting Act offered hope that a new era in stream protection was beginning in Pennsylvania. The preamble to the Desilting Act states that "it is a fundamental public right to require streams to be reasonably free of pollution and other objectionable forms of contamination."[394] This language echoes Judge Kun's 1944 decision that cleared the way for the City of Philadelphia to take legal action against coal companies for polluting the Schuylkill:

> "[N]othing is more fundamental than the right of the people to have the public streams from which they draw their water supply, free from pollution. That right is supreme, for the simple reason that health and life itself depend on it."[395]

But the affirmation of this fundamental public right in the Schuylkill River Desilting Act was something new.

In response to the State's action, the City of Philadelphia committed to upgrades to its treatment system[396] and waited to see the results of the Schuylkill River Project.

Certainly cleaning up drinking water for millions of Pennsylvanians was an important selling point for the Schuylkill River Project, but not the only one:

> "One of the greatest health hazards of America is the pollution of our streams," the Governor [Duff] thundered. "Forty-four out of each 100 of our youth were rejected for military duty in World War II. How are we to have sufficient strong men to protect our country if we do not protect the health of all?"[397]

And protecting water for all included protecting water for industry. Not only was one third of Pennsylvania's population dependent upon the Schuylkill for drinking water. "...Governor Duff pointed to the Schuylkill River, 'along whose waters one-third of the industry of Pennsylvania is found.' "[398]

Duff wasn't just interested in clean water for existing industry. The water resource investigations undertaken in conjunction with the Schuylkill River Project included providing information on water quality to encourage industries to locate facilities in the very watershed the project was working to clean up.[399]

For Duff, clean streams were necessary not only to protect public health, they were also essential to the prosperity and security of post-war Pennsylvania. And so the Schuylkill, which had been the worst river, was also the first to be cleaned up. Work to clean other rivers soon followed as Duff and his administration forced Pennsylvania to break with the polluting practices of the past.

As of February 1949, the careless discharge of coal wastes to the Schuylkill River from active cleaning operations was finally stopped.[400] But sewage discharges were not. Nor were industrial discharges stopped. Other activities on the landscape that harmed the health of the Schuylkill River continued as well.

The tightening of regulations in the years since the Schuylkill River Project has reduced some impacts. But the causes of the river's pollution have always been complicated. This, together with the river's long history of abuse, means the effects of the practices that pollute the river can still be felt today, even long after the polluting impacts are stopped.

Sewage Treatment

In conjunction with the dredging, the Sanitary Water Board ordered communities along the Schuylkill's upper reaches to treat sewage before discharging it to the River by 1951.[401] Sewage and industrial wastes required regulation and would have to meet certain standards. As of 1944, fewer than 300 sewage treatment plants had been built in all Pennsylvania[402] so it is not surprising that many of communities in the Schuylkill's headwaters had not previously been treating their sewage.

The imperative to change was met with resistance not only in the Schuylkill's headwaters. Some communities did not comply until years, even decades, later.[403] Many of these communities simply did not have money to build treatment plants.[404] The Sanitary Water Board, and its successors, would struggle for decades to balance the requirements for sewage treatment with the financial burden those requirements placed on the small communities in the Schuylkill's headwaters.

In 1966, Pennsylvania's Sewage Facilities Act, also known as Act 537, was passed. Act 537 requires municipalities to plan and regulate community and individual sewage systems. This places the responsibility for malfunctioning on-lot systems, overburdened treatment plants, and sewer lines squarely on municipalities.

In 1968, the Sanitary Water Board filed legal action against two Schuylkill headwaters communities, Middleport and New Philadelphia, for their failure to stop discharging untreated sewage into the Schuylkill River.[405] Nearly 40 years later, a public sewer system was finally available for these and neighboring communities when the system operated by the Schuylkill Valley Sewer Authority became operational in 2006. This system replaced wildcat sewers,[406] which collect sewage from one or more dwellings and discharge it untreated to waterways. The Schuylkill Valley Sewer Authority finally provided a public sewer system for 1,500 customers. The project was recognized in 2008 with the U.S. Environmental Protection Agency's Pisces Award, presented for the construction of a regional wastewater treatment plant that provides regional benefits.

> The EPA commended the authority for developing a "cost-effective, regional solution to the public health risks of direct discharge sewers that provides a long-term solution for wastewater and stormwater treatment in the Schuylkill Valley."[407]

Installing sewage treatment systems did not place financial burdens only on municipalities. Individuals who hook up to public sewer must also bear this burden. The ability to pay these costs, whether in the past or today, can weigh especially hard in communities with struggling economies. In 1932, to ease the financial burden to a property owner required to connect to public sewer, 32 McAdoo property owners were allowed to dig their own laterals, "Women 60 years of age and more are all down in the trench with girls, men and boys and all sling picks and shovels with a vim." [408] In 2011, 60 Tamaqua residents asked for a referendum that would have allowed the Borough to take out a loan in order to provide financial relief to residents for the costs of connecting to public sewer.[409] Many of these property owners had been paying sewer bills and were unaware their homes were not already connected. The referendum was ultimately defeated.[410]

Sewage discharges are a continuing problem in the Schuylkill River watershed and not just in the river's headwaters. Many treatment plants were built in the 1950s in response to Sanitary Water Board orders. Facilities were upgraded to meet requirements of the federal Clean Water Act after its passage in 1972, but many sewage treatment plants and their piping systems are old and in need of repair. Communities like the City of Reading, which once set the standard for sewage treatment now struggle to get back into compliance with state and federal regulations.[411]

An agency can order a community to treat its sewage, but what is the agency to do when the community can't, or won't, comply? Addressing sewage treatment needs in the Schuylkill River watershed is still an important issue today. Our sewage treatment infrastructure is aging at a time when municipal expenditures on new plants is unlikely, and money for upgrades and repairs is limited. Where private companies operate sewage treatment systems, costs are still a factor for those with limited ability to pay.

Efforts like the Schuylkill Action Network, a partnership among federal and state agencies, local governments, water suppliers, and watershed organizations are helping to secure funds and implement projects aimed at protecting the Schuylkill as a source of drinking water. But the Schuylkill's sewage treatment needs easily run into the hundreds of millions. As long as we discharge our sewage to our waterways, the health of our rivers will depend on how much we are willing to spend on sewage treatment.

Oil Spills

Adding to the Schuylkill River's problems were some forms of pollution that the Schuylkill River Project did nothing to address. Oil refining on the Schuylkill dates back to the 1860s and, like the other industries of that time, the refinery waste was dumped into the river.[412] Pollutants in the Schuylkill have caught fire, and the river burned on at least two occasions, the first was in 1892.[413] A second fire occurred just shortly after the official completion of the Schuylkill River Project.

> [A] seaman lost his life on the tug *Arthur N. Herron*, which, on the night of November 18, 1952, while towing a scow on the Schuylkill River in Philadelphia, caught fire when an open-flame kerosene lamp on the deck of the scow ignited highly inflammable vapors lying above an extensive accumulation of petroleum products spread over the surface of the river. Several oil refineries and facilities for oil storage, and for loading and unloading petroleum products, are located along the banks of the Schuylkill River.[414]

The residue of more than a century of oil refining remains a factor in the health of the lower Schuylkill today. In 1876, Joseph Leidy, pioneering protozoologist, documented contamination of the Schuylkill's sediments from oil refining.[415]

> [W]e found the sediments of the river, everywhere from the city to the mouth of the Schuylkill, imbued with oil, derived from the waste of the gas-works and oil refineries, so that no living thing could exist.

Groundwater under the South Philadelphia refineries is contaminated with petro-chemicals and heavy metals including lead and arsenic. Since 1997 when groundwater pumping began as part of an environmental cleanup, over 250,000 gallons of petro-chemicals have been recovered.[416]

In 1953, less than two years after the official conclusion of the Schuylkill River Project, the lower river suffered the impacts of an oil spill that extended three miles.[417] In 1970, at least three million gallons of oil spilled into the river from a refinery near Douglassville in Berks County, but the largest oil spill on the Schuylkill occurred in June 1972 when nearly eight million gallons of waste oil and sludge poured into the Schuylkill from the same Douglassville operation in the wake of Hurricane Agnes.[418] At the time, this spill was labeled the worst inland oil spill in U.S. history. Forty miles of river were impacted. These spills resulted in the Schuylkill's dubious distinction as the training ground for spill cleanup; lessons learned here helped inform response to oil spills that followed in other parts of the country.[419]

Sedimentation

Coal wastes that were discharged into the Schuylkill is the river's long acknowledged sediment problem, Even though the active discharge of coal wastes has been stopped, the river's headwaters carry a burden of coal silt. To this day, the desilting basins are still catching silt washing out of culm banks, albeit the percentage of coal wastes in the trapped sediments is much lower than during the Schuylkill River Project or even in the years immediately following it.

But soils washed from bare ground, farm fields, and development sites have also contributed to the river's sediment load. Although Duff did not address the problem of sedimentation resulting "from unscientific farming" and "improper deforestation," as extensively as he did the problem of coal wastes and sewage, he regularly included the topic among the pollution problems threatening Pennsylvania's rivers.[420]

> "In America we unfortunately had the habit of using the richest soil, then moving on across the country as it started to wear out. We have used it all now and what we have left must last forever."[421]

Duff's perspective on erosion looked not at its impact upon the streams it polluted, but on the agricultural lands left worse for the loss of soil, not an uncommon view at the time.[422] This perspective can also be seen in earlier court cases where farmers were readily compensated for lands harmed by the deposit of coal silt,[423] but where securing compensation for impacts to drinking water supplies was more difficult.[424]

But soil erosion has certainly contributed to the Schuylkill's problems.

> It is of interest to note that in the lower Schuylkill Valley, where the anthracite mines are blamed for ruining the stream, analysis shows that almost half of the material dredged from the river is not refuse from the mines—it is the much more valuable soil from our farms and hillsides.[425]

The loss of forests in the Schuylkill River watershed, lamented in 1885[426] for the negative impact on infiltration, failed to acknowledge the loss of soil that would have accompanied the deforestation.

> In the eastern United States, sediment yields have varied from about 100 tons per square mile per year (38.6 tons per square kilometer) or less in presettlement time...to 600 to 800 tons per square mile per year where land is in crops.[427]

By contrast—after the Schuylkill River Project and the construction of the desilting basins—the sediment yield at Auburn was measured at 30 tons per square mile and 39 tons per square mile at Berne. At the same time the sediment yield as measured at Manayunk in Philadelphia was 350 tons per square mile,[428] suggesting additional sediment inputs were coming from the agricultural lands and developing areas below the coal regions.

For the eastern U.S., the highest sediment yields usually have resulted from construction activities.[429] Yields of 1,000 to 5,000 tons per square mile or more rival the pre-Schuylkill River Project sediment yields for the Schuylkill's headwaters: 4,580 tons per square mile at Landingville; 3,550 tons per square mile at Berne; and 10,000 tons per square mile at South Tamaqua along the Little Schuylkill.

The characteristics of soils in the Schuylkill River's watershed, topography, and our management of the landscape affect the volume of sediment that ends up in our streams. In 1974, levels of sediment yield for two similar Schuylkill tributary watersheds, the Perkiomen and the Wissahickon, were found to differ widely. The more undeveloped Perkiomen yielded 210 tons per square mile where the neighboring and urbanizing Wissahickon yielded 780 tons per square mile.[430] That is not to say that the Perkiomen has not had its problems with erosion. Erosion in the Perkiomen was described in 1909:

> The area [Perkiomen Creek watershed] is mostly in farmland under a high state of cultivation, the original forest growth having been almost entirely cut away. The stream is subject to very sudden freshets, and during heavy rains large quantities of surface soil are eroded.[431]

Clearly eroded soils below the coal fields have also contributed to the Schuylkill's sediment load and impacted its health. Preventing soil erosion would seem to be the best cause of action to protect the river and erosion and sediment control regulations enacted since the 1974 studies have done a great deal to reduce construction site erosion. But recent monitoring suggests there is more that must be done.

Under a requirement of the Clean Water Act, the Department of Environmental Protection undertakes regular assessments of the health of Pennsylvania waters and reports those results. When a stream is found to no longer be able to support the uses for which it is classified (e.g., aquatic life, water supply, recreation, navigation), that stream is then reported as impaired.

In Pennsylvania's *Integrated Water Quality Monitoring and Assessment Report,* drafted for 2012, more than 300 stream segments, totaling more than 400 miles in the Schuylkill River watershed are listed as impaired for siltation.[432] This number *excludes* those Schuylkill tributary streams listed as impaired for siltation caused by mining. The causes of the impairment listing for these 300 plus stream segments include agriculture, erosion of derelict land, removal of vegetation, habitat modification, channelization, road runoff, land development, construction, small residential runoff, urban runoff, and golf courses.

As of 1959, Pennsylvania was still committing $500,000 every two years toward continued dredging of the Schuylkill with $300,000 to $400,000 of those funds earmarked just for the Felix pool.[433] The days when the legislature was approving multimillion dollar appropriations to address the Schuylkill sediment problems may have been over, but the idea that the Schuylkill needed continued dredging persisted. And there are those living along the Schuylkill today who call for its dredging once again.

Perhaps the Schuylkill River Project was seen as so successfully reducing the volume of sediment in the past that dredging has become viewed as the solution to any sediment load problems resulting from our actions on the landscape. Contributing to this perception is an interesting shift in terminology. The Schuylkill River Project Engineers oversaw the construction of three desilting pools as well as repairs to Felix Dam that allowed its impoundment to serve for a short time as a desilting pool. Although other dams were left along the Schuylkill, they were not considered by the Schuylkill River Project Engineers to be desilting pools, even if they do act as sediment traps. But by 1985, every impoundment behind every dam along the Schuylkill was described as a desilting pool in agency documents.[434]

But a reliance on dredging misses the lesson of the Schuylkill River Project. Stopping the discharge of coal waste marked the turning point for the river, the turning point that made the cleanup possible. And if the discharge of coal waste could be stopped in the 1940s, it is well past time for the impairment of streams by soil erosion to be stopped as well.

Dam Removal

Constructing a dam on a river creates a sediment trap. As the river slows behind the dam, silt, debris, and nutrients become trapped in the waters of the impoundment. Over time, the impoundment can fill with the sediment.

This had been the very purpose behind the construction of Auburn and Kernsville dams and the Tamaqua weir and the repairs to Felix Dam. But an impoundment filling with sediment isn't necessarily compatible with recreation, especially the power boating, water skiing, and personal water craft that would come to use the dams like Felix that remained on the river.

> In spots that were solid islands of oily culm, flotillas of speed boats ride with 15 or 20 feet of water under their hulls. And fishermen, from youngsters with bent-pin rigs to adults with fancy fresh-water outfits, were out in force.[435]

Indeed, making navigation possible was the reason dams were built along the river in the first place, the reason why Schuylkill Navigation had maintained a slack water system that included 32 dams. Recreation activities did develop along the dam pools afterward; however, power boats and personal watercraft would not have been at home on the river before the Schuylkill Navigation system.

As the old Schuylkill Navigation dams trapped sediment, coal waste filled the channel and flood heights increased. Even before the Schuylkill River Project, officials representing the City of Reading had proposed removal of the old Schuylkill Navigation dams.

> City Engineer Robert S. Chubb has proposed the removal of these three dams [Kissinger, Poplar Neck, and Klapperthal or Big Reading] as a method of dropping the level of the water and increasing the speed of the Schuylkill's flow so that some of the culm and silt would be washed away. The effect of this washing would be, Chubb feels, to lower the bed of the stream as well as the water level.[436]

Chubb, like the Schuylkill River Project Engineers, understood that removing dams could restore more natural flows and move the coal waste that had accumulated behind the Schuylkill Navigation dams.

People who lived along the Schuylkill had long called for the removal of the accumulated coal waste, but once the dredging was begun in earnest in 1948, some began to call for preservation of the very dams that had slowed the river's flow and caused the coal wastes to settle out.

> Once cleaned of its filth, this "lake," more than a mile in length, could be one of Reading's most valuable recreational assets because hundreds of feet of city-owned land are located along its eastern shore. But [Leisz's Dam] is doomed to destruction.[437]

A Schuylkill River Recreation Council was formed to push for new dams to provide pools for recreation, concerned that swimming and boating opportunities would be lost.[438] With the Schuylkill Navigation dams on the river since the early 1800s, there was no memory of the Schuylkill without dams. And there was little or no understanding among the general public about how dam removal benefited river systems.

Department of Forests and Waters Deputy Secretary McCawley seemed to have little sympathy for those wanting to preserve dams targeted for removal under the Schuylkill River Project, "It boils down to the fact that Reading can't have its cake and penny, too."[439]

McCawley was not unsympathetic to local residents wishing to bring back long-lost recreation opportunities, but he made it clear that providing recreation was not part of the Department of Forests and Waters' mandate for the river cleanup.

> The deputy secretary also stressed that "the provision of recreational facilities is nowhere stated as an objective of the legislation concerning the river cleanup project. Actually recreational facilities will be a by-product of the project."[440]

If Reading wanted a dam, the City would have to build it. The State was not going to do so.

The argument over Leisz's Dam presaged future user conflicts that would focus on dams. Moreover, the Schuylkill River Project was directly responsible for one such conflict when repairs were made to Felix Dam to preserve its use as a desilting pool for five to 10 more years.[441] But Felix Dam was removed only recently on November 1st, 2007, after a major breach in 1978, a series of temporary repairs, and then another major breach in September 1999.

After the 1999 breach, some local residents and the Felix Dam Preservation Association worked to see the dam repaired. Other local residents like Robert J. Smith of Muhlenberg Township, recreation organizations like the Keystone Canoe Club, and watershed organizations like the Delaware Riverkeeper Network argued for a free-flowing Schuylkill River. Supporters of a dam removal ultimately won the day.

As a remnant of the Schuylkill River Project, Felix Dam was owned by the Commonwealth, but removing the dam required a permit from the U.S. Army Corps of Engineers. This permitting process took nearly 10 years.

Even though Felix Dam wasn't removed until 2007, the fight over its removal helped spark other dam removal efforts in the Schuylkill River watershed. Dams removed since 1999 include Manatawny Creek Dam (2000), Collegeville Dam on the Perkiomen Creek (2003), Mirror Lake Dam on the Wyomissing Creek (2004), Charming Forge Dam on the Tulpehocken Creek (2004), Goodrich Dam on the Perkiomen Creek (2005), Mohnton Creek Dam (2006), Nestle Dam on Pigeon Creek (2007), and the Schuylkill's Vincent and Plymouth Dams (2009).

Impounding Basins to Parks

When impounding basins were constructed along the Schuylkill's banks to hold the dredged sediments, there was criticism that the pollution from coal wastes had just been moved from the Schuylkill to its riverbanks. In the upper reaches of the watershed, coal deposited by the river along its banks had made some lands useless. It would not have been unreasonable to wonder what use these lands would have even after all marketable coal was reclaimed.

But interest in the lands that were acquired for the Schuylkill River Project emerged almost immediately. Some inquiries—such as planting trees along the property line[442]—related to the concerns of neighbors suddenly finding the Commonwealth of Pennsylvania pumping tons of dredged sediments into a huge impounding basin next door. A request for space for a garden was considered a compatible use[443] as was a water storage basin for irrigation.[444]

The basins provided an unmatched location for small unit tactical training and demonstration of Army tactics for cadets at Valley Forge Military Academy.[445]

As coal was reclaimed, the Department of Forests and Waters also began to consider what to do with the lands it had pushed so hard to acquire just a few years before. Some of the lands upon which the impounding basins were built were only leased, not owned. The use of those lands, like the Norristown impounding basin, was returned to the property owner as soon as dredging was complete.[446]

Just as the Schuylkill River Desilting Act empowered the Department of Forests and Waters, through the Water and Power Resources Board, to acquire land, it also empowered the agency to sell, with the approval of the governor, those lands.[447] A few small parcels were sold to fire companies.[448] The Harmonville impounding basin was never used to hold dredged sediments and was sold.[449] No sign of it can be seen on the landscape. A housing development now sits where the basin was.

The Spring Mill impounding basin was sold to the National Label Company, but 54 acres of the basin were donated by the company to Whitemarsh Township. The National Label Company developed portions of the site, but the land owned by Whitemarsh Township, known as Kline Park, is preserved as wooded, passive use open space.[450] Like the Spring Mill basin, many of these lands that might have been made useless by their use as impounding basins are providing benefits to surrounding communities today.

Upper Merion Township acquired both the North and Middle Abrams impounding basins. North Abrams has been developed as the popular Heuser Park athletic complex with football and baseball fields, a playground, and a clubhouse.[451] Middle Abram has been developed as Bob Case Park.

The Valley Forge impounding basins were transferred to the National Park Service in 1982 and are now part of Valley Forge National Historic Park.

In 1981, 3.5 acres of the Black Rock impounding basin site were conveyed to the Pennsylvania Fish and Boat Commission for a boat ramp and parking lot. In 1990, the remainder of the site, roughly 120 acres, was conveyed to Chester County. The site has been developed as Black Rock Sanctuary with wetland, woodland, and meadow habitats. A 3/4-mile interpretive trail has been created which showcases these habitats. The site has been designated an Important Bird Area by the National Audubon Society.[452]

Chester County also acquired the Linfield and Sanatoga impounding basins. Black Rock Sanctuary and the Linfield and Sanatoga County Preserves are administered by Chester County Facilities and Parks.[453]

Montgomery County acquired the Oaks Reach of the Schuylkill Canal, Lock 60, and Mingo impounding basin in 2010.[454]

The Birdsboro impounding basin was conveyed to Union Township in 1989. Recently the Township has unveiled improvements to the site including a two-mile loop trail around the basin, pedestrian bridges over the Schuylkill Navigation canal, a picnic pavilion, and a boat ramp to the river.[455]

The South Seyfert impounding basin was acquired by Exeter Township and has been developed as the Trout Run Sports Complex offering football, soccer, and baseball fields.

The Riverside impounding basin along with the canal lock, stone warehouse, and parking area associated with Felix Dam were conveyed to Muhlenberg Township in 1982. At this time, the basin is maintained as wooded, passive use open space.

In 1982, the Eplers impounding basin was transferred to the Pennsylvania Fish and Boat Commission. A recreation area, boat launch, and parking area have been developed.

Even the Kernsville impounding basin, constructed for the dredged spoils from the Kernsville pool, has become a day-use park, the Kernsville Dam Recreation Area. The non-profit Blue Mountain Wildlife, Inc., a Hamburg area citizens group, has leased the land from the Department of Environmental Protection, which owns the land.[456] Blue Mountain Wildlife was organized in response to a proposal for intense development of active use recreation facilities. As a result of the efforts of Blue Mountain Wildlife and its local supporters, the area is preserved as a passive recreation area and includes three miles of trails and access to the Schuylkill River.[457]

Some of the impounding basins remain in state ownership with work on-going to reclaim coal. Sites like the basin at Oaks are being eyed for potential recreation opportunities and linkages with other open space they might provide. The Department of Environmental Protection has no plans to sell land or facilities associated with the Auburn and Tamaqua desilting pools, but these have also had use agreements with local organizations providing recreational opportunities.

These impounding basin lands could have been sold for development. Between the time of their acquisition and when the Department of Environmental Resources began looking at selling the properties in the 1980s, land use had changed around many of the facilities.

> Several basins have been almost entirely surrounded by suburban and residential development. Depending on one's perspective, the basins become valuable or increased residential development if sold to private residential developers, or desilting project lands become increasingly valuable as greenbelt and recreation areas surrounded by burgeoning population centers, and thus provide respite from the more heavily developed suburban areas.[458]

Although the impounding basin lands might have been sold for development, another Schuylkill River "first" required the Department of Environmental Resources to consider uses that would preserve these lands for open space, recreation, and conservation.

In 1978, the Schuylkill River was named Pennsylvania's first Scenic River. The legislation that made this possible was the Pennsylvania Scenic River Act[459] was passed in 1972 in response the federal Wild and Scenic Rivers System created by Congress in 1968.[460] Damming rivers for economic benefit has a long history, but during the 20th Century, the dams had been getting bigger and their impacts on rivers more widely recognized. By 1972, the understanding of the environmental benefits of free-flowing streams was increasing and the Pennsylvania Scenic River Act and the federal Wild and Scenic Rivers Act encouraged the preservation of free-flowing streams.

Implementation of the Pennsylvania Scenic River Act was begun with a task force undertaking an inventory of streams eligible for designation. Over 200 waterways were identified as candidates,[461] but just three rose to the top for consideration as the stream to be designated as Pennsylvania's first Scenic River: Pine Creek from Ansonia to its confluence with the Susquehanna; the Lehigh River from the Francis E. Walter Dam to Jim Thorpe; and the Schuylkill from Port Clinton to the Fairmount Dam in Philadelphia.[462]

A prime force in the Schuylkill's consideration was a relatively new environmental organization, the Schuylkill River Greenway Association, which was chaired by Ferdinand K. Thun. A son of one of the founders of the Berkshire Knitting Mills, Thun was a community leader, local philanthropist, and a conservationist. Thun's advocacy for the Schuylkill carried weight, but the case for the Schuylkill's nomination was made in a report prepared by the Pennsylvania Environmental Council for the Department of Environmental Resources.

To prepare its report, the Pennsylvania Environmental Council formed the Schuylkill River Study Committee which walked the shorelines, paddled the river, and documented the Schuylkill's characteristics and its eligibility to be designated as a wild, scenic, pastoral, recreational, or modified recreational river per the requirements of the Pennsylvania Scenic River Act.[463]

The legislation establishing the Schuylkill as Pennsylvania's first Scenic River, P.L. 1415, No. 333, was signed by Governor Milton J. Shapp on November 28, 1978.[464] Over time, legislation would be passed to add portions of the West Branch Schuylkill River, portions of the Little Schuylkill, and the main stem Schuylkill from the Norristown Dam to Spring Mill Creek which had been excluded from that first scenic river legislation.

The designation of the Schuylkill as a Scenic River made protection, rather than development, a priority for the lands of the Schuylkill River Project. Whether the Department of Environmental Resources, and later the Department of Environmental Protection, kept these lands or sold them, they were to be managed in a way that enhanced the scenic nature of the Schuylkill River.

The next chapter

It is time to write the next chapter in the history of the Schuylkill River; it will be written by those who will make today's river management decisions.

In the past, the Schuylkill was allowed to become this country's dirtiest river because of a round robin of finger pointing. No discharger could be made to stop polluting the river as long as another was allowed to continue. But committed advocates of clean streams like Grover Ladner and Jim Duff brought that era to an end. The Schuylkill River Project marked a break with the past and the beginning of a new era in river protection.

But the Schuylkill needs—as do all our rivers—her advocates still. The false choice of economy versus environment that was reflected in the 1886 *Pennsylvania Coal Company v. Sanderson* case is being used again today to justify decisions about how our rivers are managed. We owe a debt to those who worked to clean up our rivers in the past. It is now our obligation to ensure that decisions about the Schuylkill's management are not made on the basis of the river's past reputation.

So get outside; experience the Schuylkill first-hand. Enjoy the river. Walk along its banks in Fairmount Park; bike the Schuylkill Trail near Pottstown. Explore the history found in the towns along the river. Hike the headwaters and find the river's source. Or paddle the river from Schuylkill Haven to Philadelphia during the next Schuylkill Sojourn.

The next chapter in the Schuylkill's history can begin with you.

We sincerely hope that the future administrations will not permit the Schuylkill River to again be despoiled…

— Schuylkill River Project Engineers, 1951[465]

Notes

1 "Duff Sees Statewide Reclamation Work." 1948. Unidentified newspaper clipping. Rosendale Papers. In possession of the author, Bristol, PA.

Bad Reputation

2 The Academy of Natural Sciences, Natural Lands Trust and The Conservation Fund. 2001. *Schuylkill Watershed Conservation Plan.* Philadelphia. Pennsylvania Department of Conservation and Natural Resources.

3 U.S. Census Bureau. *State and County QuickFacts.* Retrieved from http://quickfacts.census.gov/qfd/states/42000.html.

4 Delaware River Basin Commission. 2008. *Delaware River. State of the Basin Report.*

5 Gallons per capita per day is calculated by dividing the residential well water use and public water supply for the population of the service area.

6 Delaware River Basin Commission. 2008. *Delaware River. State of the Basin Report.*

7 Kauffman, G.J. 2011. *Economic Value of the Delaware Estuary Watershed.* Partnership for the Delaware Estuary, Inc.

8 Berks Conservancy. 2011. *The Business of Nature: The Return on Environment in Berks County.*

9 Pennsylvania Fish and Boat Commission. *Schuylkill River American Shad.* Retrieved from http://fishandboat.com/shad_schu.htm.

10 Miller, L.M., et al. 2010. *Migratory Fish Management and Restoration Plan for the Susquehanna River Basin.* Susquehanna River Anadromous Fish Restoration Cooperative.

11 Philadelphia Water Department. *News Stream.* Retrieved from http://www.phillywatersheds.org/category/blog-tags/news-stream?page=6.

12 Schuylkill Navy. 2012. *2012 Regatta Schedule.* Retrieved from http://boathouserow.org.lsh0102.uslec.net/sked12.html.

13 Van Allen, P. 14 April 2010. Aberdeen Asset Management to Sponsor Dad Vail Regatta in Phila. Through 2013. *Philadelphia Business Journal.* Retrieved from http://www.bizjournals.com/philadelphia/stories/2010/04/12/daily18.html.

14 Brown, L. 6 October 2001. 2001 Houston Dragon Boat Festival Address. *Texas Dragon Boat Association.* Retrieved from http://www.texasdragonboat.com/news/2001/20011006.asp.

15 Berks Conservancy. 2011. *The Business of Nature: The Return on*

Environment in Berks County.

16 Kramek, N. and Loh, L. 2007. *The History of Philadelphia's Water Supply and Sanitation System.* Retrieved from http://esa.un.org/iys/docs/san_lib_docs/Philalessonsinsustainability%5B1%5D.pdf.

17 Younger, L. 2004. *A Bridge to the Future: Fairmount Park Strategic Plan - Summary Report.* Leon Younger and PROS for Fairmount Park and the City of Philadelphia. Retrieved from http://www.fairmountpark.org/pdf/FPC_Summary_Report.pdf.

18 Schuylkill River Development Council. n.d. FAQ. *Schuylkill Banks.* Retrieved from http://www.schuylkillbanks.org/about/faq.

19 Schuylkill River National and State Heritage Area. 2008. *A Shared Commons.* Retrieved from http://www.schuylkillriver.org/newsletters/2008_4_Fall.pdf.

20 Carter van Dyke Associates, et al. 2011. *A Plan for Compatible Economic Development of the Middle Schuylkill.* Retrieved from http://www.schuylkillhighlands.org/Resources/Documents/Schuylkill%20CED%20Plan%202011_low%20res.pdf.

21 PennPraxis. 2012. Lower Schuylkill Master Plan Meetings in April. *Plan Philly.* Retrieved from http://planphilly.com/lowerschuylkill.

22 Latrobe, B.H. 1799. *View of the Practicability and Means of Supplying the City of Philadelphia with Wholesome Water. In a Letter to John Miller, Esquire, from B. Henry Latrobe, Engineer. December 29th, 1798.* Corporation of Philadelphia. Philadelphia: Zachariah Poulson, Jr. Retrieved from http://www.phillyh2o.org/backpages/PDFs_Misc/ogden_03.pdf.

The Country's Dirtiest River

23 Latrobe. 1799. *op. cit.*

24 Gibson, J.M. Last Modified: 12 April 2006. Water for the City. *Clean Water for Life.* Retrieved from http://www.phillyh2o.org/backpages/MSB_Water.htm.

25 Fairmount Water Works Interpretive Center. n.d. *About the Fairmount Water Works.* Retrieved from http://www.fairmountwaterworks.org/about.php?sec=3.

26 Cresson, C.M. 1875. *Results of Examinations of Water from the River Schuylkill. Communication by request to Dr. W. H. McFadden , Chief Engineer of the Water Department of the City of Philadelphia.* Philadelphia: Wm. Mann. Retrieved from http://archive.org/.

27 Hagner, C. 1869. *Early History of the Falls of Schuylkill, Manayunk, Schuylkill and Lehigh Navigation Companies, Fairmount Waterworks, Etc.*

Philadelphia: Claxton, Remsen, and Haffelfinger. Retrieved from http://archive.org/.

28 Cresson. 1875. *op. cit.*

29 *Ibid.*

30 *Ibid.*

31 Keyser, C. S. and Cochran, T. 1886. *Lemon Hill and Fairmount Park: the papers of Charles S. Keyser and Thomas Cochran, relative to a public park for Philadelphia.* Philadelphia: Horace J. Smith. Originals published in 1856 and 1872. Retrieved from http://books.google.com/.

32 "The Schuylkill Poisoned: Thousands of Fish Floating on the Stream." 10 July, 1882. *New York Times.* Retrieved from http://www.nytimes.com/ref/membercenter/nytarchive.html.

33 "A Lesson in Forestry." 18 September 1885. *New York Times.* Retrieved from http://www.nytimes.com/ref/membercenter/nytarchive.html.

34 "Typhoid and Polluted Water." 16 April 1891. *New York Times.* Retrieved from http://www.nytimes.com/ref/membercenter/nytarchive.html.

35 "The River Set on Fire." 2 November 1892. *New York Times.* Retrieved from http://www.nytimes.com/ref/membercenter/nytarchive.html.

36 Ludlow, W. 15 April 1885. *The Future Water Supply of Philadelphia.* Presented at the meeting of the Franklin Institute, Philadelphia. Reprinted in *The Sanitarian.* 1885. Vol. 15. 106-120. New York: Medico-Legal Society. Retrieved from http://books.google.com/.

37 Hazen, A. 1896. *A Practical Plan for Sand Filtration in Philadelphia.* Journal of the Franklin Institute, 142(847): 366-385. Philadelphia: Franklin Institute. Retrieved from http://books.google.com/.

38 Ludlow. 1885. *op. cit.*

39 Water Supply Commission of Pennsylvania. 1916. *Water Resources Inventory Report, Part X: Culm in the Streams of the Anthracite Region.* Harrisburg, PA: Wm. Stanley Ray. Retrieved from http://books.google.com/.

Stone Coal

40 Shultz, C. H., ed. 1999. *The Geology of Pennsylvania.* Lebanon, PA: Pennsylvania Department of Conservation and Natural Resources, Bureau of Topographic and Geologic Survey and Pittsburgh Geological Society.

41 Edmunds, W.E. 2002. *Educational Series 7: Coal in Pennsylvania.* Pennsylvania Geological Survey. Retrieved from http://www.dcnr.state.pa.us/topogeo/education/coal/es7.pdf.

42 U.S. Energy Information Administration. 2010. *Recoverable Coal Reserves*

at Producing Mines, Estimated Recoverable Reserves, and Demonstrated Reserve Base by Mining Method, 2010. Retrieved from http://www.eia.gov/coal/annual/pdf/table15.pdf.

43 U.S. Energy Information Administration. 2011. *Annual Energy Outlook 2011 with Projections to 2035.* Retrieved from http://electricdrive.org/index.php?ht=a/GetDocumentAction/id/27843.

44 Blaschak Coal Corporation. 2012. *Blaschak Coal Corporation Sets Coal Mine Production and Sales Record in 2011; Anticipates Record 1 Million Tons of Production in 2012.* Retrieved from http://www.blaschakcoal.com/wp-content/uploads/Blaschak-Record-Year-Outlook-for-2012-1.9.12-FINAL.pdf.

45 Fox Davies Capital. 2 May 2012. *Fw: Views from the Trading Floor - Featuring Falkland Oil & Gas, Sefton Resources, Premier Gold Resources and Edenville Energy 2nd May.* Retrieved from http://www.proactiveinvestors.co.uk/columns/fox-davies-capital/9214/fw-views-from-the-trading-floor-featuring-falkland-oil-gas-sefton-resources-premier-gold-resources-and-edenville-energy-2nd-may-9214.html.

46 Yancey, H.F. and Fraser, T. 1929. *Coal Washing Investigations: Methods and Tests.* U.S. Department of Commerce, Bureau of Mines.

47 Commonwealth of Pennsylvania. 1898. *Report of the Commission Appointed to Investigate the Waste of Coal Mining with the View to the Utilizing of the Waste.* Philadelphia: Allen, Lane & Scott's Printing House.

48 "Culm Burner Designed To Heat New State Prison at Frackville." 27 January 1985. *Reading Eagle.* Retrieved from http://news.google.com/.

49 U.S. Department of Energy. 2007. *Final Environmental Impact Statement for the Gilberton Coal-To-Clean Fuels and Power Project, Gilberton, Pennsylvania, Volume 1: Main Text.* Retrieved from http://energy.gov/sites/prod/files/nepapub/nepa_documents/RedDont/EIS-0357-FEIS-01-2007.pdf.

50 Wheelabrator Technologies. n.d. *Wheelabrator Frackville Plant Facts.* Retrieved from http://www.wheelabratortechnologies.com. Retrieved from http://www.wheelabratortechnologies.com/plants/independent-power/wheelabrator-frackville/.

51 Wells, S.W. 1989. *The Schuylkill Navigation and the Girard Canal.* Thesis, University of Pennsylvania. Philadelphia. Retrieved from http://archive.org/.

52 "In Retrospect: 50 Years Ago. August 13, 1898" 13 August 1948. *Pottstown Mercury.* Retrieved from http://search.ancestry.com/.

53 Water Supply Commission of Pennsylvania. 1916. *op. cit.*

54 *Ibid.*

55 *Ibid.*

56 "Mining Coal from the Schuylkill's Bed." 11 August 1901. *Reading Eagle*. Retrieved from http://news.google.com/.

57 U.S. Department of Commerce. 1907. *Bulletin of the Department of Labor – XIV*. Washington: Government Printing Office. Retrieved from http://books.google.com/.

58 "Use 'River Coal' from Reading and Vicinity." 11 August 1901. *Reading Eagle*. Retrieved from http://news.google.com/.

59 Water Supply Commission of Pennsylvania. 1916. *op. cit.*

60 Webbert, C.W. 1920. *River and Creek Coal in Eastern Pennsylvania. Bulletin No. 6*. Commonwealth of Pennsylvania, Department of Internal Affairs, Topographic and Geologic Survey. Retrieved from http://www.libraries.psu.edu/content/dam/psul/up/emsl/documents/pags_reports/no.103.pdf.

61 Sisler, J. D. 1928. Bulletin No. 92: *Anthracite Culm and Silt*. Commonwealth of Pennsylvania, Department of Internal Affairs, Topographic and Geologic Survey.

62 Biesecker, J.E., et al. 1968. *Water Resources of the Schuylkill River Basin*. U.S Department of the Interior, Geological Survey for the Commonwealth of Pennsylvania, Department of Forests and Waters.

63 *Ibid.*

64 *Ibid.*

65 Schuylkill River Project Engineers. 1951. *The Schuylkill River Desilting Project: Final Report of the Schuylkill River Project Engineers*. Commonwealth of Pennsylvania, Department of Forests and Waters, Water and Power Resources Board.

66 "Phila. Is Disgusted with 'Coal Cocktails.' " 15 March 1940. *Reading Eagle*. Retrieved from http://news.google.com/.

67 Wolf. B. 7 July 1949. "They're Cleaning Up Pennsylvania's Foulest River." *Saturday Evening Post*, 222(2): 20-21, 44, 47, 49-50. Retrieved from http://www.schuylkillwaters.org/news_files/07091949saturdayeveningpost.pdf.

68 "A Great City's Water Supply," 20 July 1885. *New York Times*. Retrieved from http://www.nytimes.com/ref/membercenter/nytarchive.html.

A Trifling Inconvenience

69 "Duff Inspects Schuylkill." 28 October 1949. *Gettysburg Times*. Retrieved from http://search.ancestry.com/.

70 Commonwealth of Pennsylvania. 1868. *Journal of the House of*

Representatives of the Commonwealth of Pennsylvania of the Session Begun in Harrisburg on the Seventh Day of January, 1868. Harrisburg, PA: Singerly and Myers. Retrieved from http://books.google.com/.

71 Simpson, W., et al. 1868. *Memorial to the Senate and House of Representatives.* Philadelphia: J.B. Chandler. Retrieved from http://www.phillyh2o.org/backpages/Schuylkill_Archive/Petition_1868_text.pdf

72 Casner, N. 1999. "Polluter Versus Polluter: The Pennsylvania Railroad and the Manufacturing of Pollution Policies in the 1920s." *Journal of Policy History,* 11(2): 179-200. 1999. Retrieved from http://journals.cambridge.org/abstract_S0898030600003195.

73 *Pennsylvania Coal Co. v. Sanderson,* 113 Pa. 126, 1886.

74 Balch, T.W. 1915. 'Arbitration' as a Term of International Law, II. *Columbia Law Review,* 15(8): 662-679. New York: Trustees of the Columbia Law Review.

75 *Pennsylvania Coal Co. v. Sanderson,* 113 Pa. 126, 1886.

76 *Ibid.*

77 Northeast Reporter, 1912. *Containing all the Decisions of the Supreme Courts of Ohio, Illinois, Indiana, Massachusetts, Appellate Court of Indiana, and Appeals Court of New York, Apr 23 – July 30, 1912. Volume 98.* Saint Paul, MN: West Publishing Company. Retrieved from http://books.google.com/.

78 Wagner, S. 1951. "Statutory Stream Pollution Control." *University of Pennsylvania Law Review.* 100(2): 225-241. 1951. Retrieved from http://www.oclc.org/firstsearch/.

79 Atlantic Reporter. 1896. *Containing all the Decisions of the Supreme Courts of Maine, New Hampshire, Vermont, Rhode Island, Connecticut, and Pennsylvania; Court of Error and Appeals, Court of Chancery, and Supreme and Prerogative Court of New Jersey, Court of Error and Appeals and Court of Chancery of Delaware; and Court of Appeals, Maryland, November 13, 1895 – March 25, 1896. Vol. 33.* Saint Paul, MN: West Publishing Company. Retrieved from http://books.google.com/.

80 *Journal of the Common Council of the City of Philadelphia from April 6, 1896, to September 24, 1896, Volume I, with an Appendix.* 1896. Philadelphia: Dunlap Printing Company. Retrieved from http://books.google.com/.

81 *Journal of the Common Council of the City of Philadelphia from October 1, 1896, to April 1, 1897, Volume II, with an Appendix.* 1897. Philadelphia: Dunlap Printing Company. Retrieved from http://archive.org/.

82 "Three Berks Farmers Sue 21 Coal Operators." 11 September 1899. *Reading Eagle.* Retrieved from http://news.google.com/

83 "$50,000 in Coal Dirt Damages for Farmers." 16 May 1901. *Reading Eagle*. Retrieved from http://news.google.com/.

84 "Another Investigation along the Schuylkill." 4 August 1905. *Reading Eagle*. Retrieved from http://news.google.com/.

85 *Ibid.*

86 "Not Accepted: Pumping Station Inspected, but the Sewer Committee Will Not Take It Off the Contractor's Hands For the Present." 24 April 1895. *Reading Eagle*. Retrieved from http://news.google.com/.

87 Spatz, D. 14 November 2010. "Maintenance a key issue for local sewage treatment plants." *Reading Eagle*. Retrieved from http://readingeagle.com/Article.aspx?id=263402.

88 Levine, A. Last Modified: 12 April 2006. "Drainage for the City." *Clean Water for Life*. Retrieved from http://www.phillyh2o.org/backpages/MSB_DRAINAGE2/MSB_DRAINAGE.htm.

89 "Warrant Ready to Pay for Fritz's Island." 25 August 1906. *Reading Eagle*. Retrieved from http://news.google.com/.

90 Schladweiler, J.C. 15 January 2002. *Tracking Down the Roots of our Sanitary Sewers*. Retrieved from http://www.sewerhistory.org/chronos/disposal.htm.

91 U.S. Bureau of Labor Statistics. n.d. *op. cit.*

92 "Will Cost $8,000,000 to End the Pollution of the Schuylkill River." 12 December 1912. *Reading Eagle*. Retrieved from http://news.google.com/.

93 Goodell, E.B. 1905. *A Review of the Laws Forbidding Pollution of Inland Waters in the United States*. Department of the Interior-U.S. Geological Survey Washington, D.C.: Government Printing Office. Retrieved from http://pubs.usgs.gov/wsp/0152/report.pdf.

94 Ladner, G.C. 1929. *If the People Will It that the Streams of Pennsylvania Shall Be Clean: It Can Be Done*. Presented at the Annual Meeting of the Pennsylvania Division, Izaak Walton League of America. 9 September 1929. Harrisburg, PA: Pennsylvania Division, Izaak Walton League of America. Retrieved from http://www.phillyh2o.org/backpages/ladner1929.htm.

95 With no regulatory authority in place to prevent pollution, cities like Philadelphia pursued legal recourse under common law claims such as nuisance and trespass.

96 Pennsylvania Water Supply Commission. 1914. *Annual Report of the Pennsylvania Water Supply Commission: 1913*. Harrisburg, PA: Wm. Stanley Ray. Retrieved from http://books.google.com/.

97 Bituminous coal, found in western Pennsylvania, is softer than anthracite and burns more readily, but contains lower percentages of carbon.

98 Ulrich, J.O., ed. 1917. *Schuylkill Legal Record Containing Cases Decided by the Judges of the Courts of Schuylkill County with the Decisions of the Supreme and Superior Courts on Appeal from Schuylkill County*. Tamaqua, PA: Record Printing Company. Retrieved from http://books.google.com/.

99 Water Supply Commission of Pennsylvania. 1916. *op. cit.*

100 *Ibid.*

101 Schuylkill River Project Engineers. 1951. *op. cit.*

102 "Reports Schuylkill is 'Dirtiest' River." 5 November 1930. *Reading Eagle*. Retrieved from http://news.google.com/.

103 "River Pollution Costly to Schuylkill Valley." 18 May 1933. *Reading Eagle*. Retrieved from http://news.google.com/.

104 Pennsylvania General Assembly, House of Representatives. 1937. *History of House bills and resolutions, with indexes to bills, resolutions, joint resolutions, acts and vetoes, together with text of veto messages. Session of 1937. Final Issue.*

105 P.L 1987, No. 394 of 1937.

106 *Ibid.*

107 Ladner, G.C. 1937. Pennsylvania's New Pure Streams Law. *Pennsylvania Angler*. 6(9): 4-5, 10-11. Retrieved from http://fishandboat.com/PaAnglerLegacyIssues.htm.

108 "Culm Chokes Fire Engines." 24 February 1941. *Reading Eagle*. Retrieved from http://news.google.com/.

109 "Restoration Group Hits Drainage Plan." 21 January 1941. *Reading Eagle*. Retrieved from http://news.google.com/.

110 "Court Airs Silt Issue." 1 July 1943. *Reading Eagle*. Retrieved from http://news.google.com/.

111 *Ibid.*

112 *Ibid.*

113 *Ibid.*

114 "Menges to Continue Fight for Clean Schuylkill River." 14 July 1943. *Reading Eagle*. Retrieved from http://news.google.com/.

115 "Start Silt Suit." 29 October 1943. *Gettysburg Times*. Retrieved from http://search.ancestry.com/.

116 "Court Refuses To Receive River Suit." 6 October 1943. *Gettysburg Times*. Retrieved from http://news.google.com/.

117 "Objections to Anti-Pollution Suit Dismissed." 23 March 1944. *Williamsport Gazette and Bulletin*. Retrieved from http://search.ancestry.com/.

118 Mock. J. 31 March 1944. "All-Outdoors: Stream Purification Wins Philadelphia Court Test." *Pittsburgh Press*. Retrieved from http://news.google.com/.

119 Schuylkill River Project Engineers. 1951. *op. cit.*

120 Pitkin, F.A. 1956. Correction of a Fluviatile Delinquent: The Schuylkill River. *Water for Industry. A Symposium Presented on December 29, 1953 at the Boston Meeting of the American Association for the Advancement of Science*. Washington, D.C: American Association for the Advancement of Science.

121 Pennsylvania General Assembly, House of Representatives. 1945. *History of House bills and resolutions, with indexes to bills, resolutions, joint resolutions, acts and vetoes, together with text of veto messages. Session of 1945. Final Issue.*

122 *Ibid.*

123 The Schuylkill River Desilting Act was also sponsored by Charles Brunner, Jr.

124 Duff, J.H. 1946. Attorney General James H. Duff Highlights Federation Convention! Stream Pollution Can No Longer Be Tolerated. *Pennsylvania Angler.* 15(4): 2, 3, 18. Retrieved from http://fishandboat.com/PaAnglerLegacyIssues.htm.

James Henderson Duff

125 "Class of 1876 Prize Debate and Oratorical Contest." 24 February 1903. *Daily Princetonian*, 27(183). Retrieved from http://theprince.princeton.edu/.

126 University of Pennsylvania Department of Law. 1906. *The American Law Register: From January to December, 1906, Volume 54.* Retrieved from http://books.google.com/.

127 Phillips, R.R. 2007. *The Phillips Family History.* Unpublished manuscript.

128 "Attorney General Denies Accusation." 7 May 1943. *Huntingdon Daily News*. Retrieved from http://search.ancestry.com/.

129 Frederick, R. 1944. *Official Opinions of the Attorney General of Pennsylvania for the Years 1943 and 1944.* Harrisburg, P: Commonwealth of Pennsylvania, Department of Justice. Retrieved from http://search.attorneygeneral.gov/.

130 *Ibid.*

131 "Sanitary Water Board Has Power To End Pollution–Martin."17 March 1944. *Connellsville Daily Courier.* Retrieved from http://search.ancestry.com/.

132 "Ending Fight on the Clarion River." 20 December 1945. *Oil City Blizzard*. Retrieved from http://search.ancestry.com/.

133 Lindgren, L.R. 21 July 1946. "Duff Pledged to Crush Foes of Clean-up." *Pittsburgh Press*. Pennsylvania State Archives. Pennsylvania Historic and Museums Commission.

134 Prior to 1968, Pennsylvania's Constitution limited governors to one four-year term.

135 Wilkes University Election Statistics Project. n.d. Pennsylvania Governors (1789-2003). *Pennsylvania Gubernatorial Election Returns:* Retrieved from http://staffweb.wilkes.edu/harold.cox/gov/indexgov.html.

136 "Ed Rendell." 21 May 2012. *BALLOTPEDIA*. Retrieved from http://ballotpedia.org/wiki/index.php/Ed_Rendell.

137 Beers, P.B. 1980. *Pennsylvania Politics Today and Yesterday: The Tolerable Accommodation*. University Park, PA: The Pennsylvania State University.

138 "Industrial Waterway Pollution Means Arrest." 5 December 1944. *Indiana Evening Gazette*. Retrieved from http://search.ancestry.com/.

An Actionable Wrong

139 "Water Board Starts Plan to Clean Streams." 16 March 1944. *Clearfield Progress*. Retrieved from http://search.ancestry.com/.

140 "Public to Be Given Chance to Discuss Pollution of Streams." 7 June 1944. *Huntingdon Daily News*. Retrieved from http://search.ancestry.com/.

141 "Urges Preparation for Purification of State's Streams." 13 October 1944. *Williamsport Gazette and Bulletin*. Retrieved from http://search.ancestry.com/.

142 "Industrial Waterway Pollution Means Arrest." 5 December 1944. *Indiana Evening Gazette*. Retrieved from http://search.ancestry.com/.

143 "State Will Set Deadline on Sewer Plants." 7 September 1945. *Bradford Era*. Retrieved from http://search.ancestry.com/.

144 "Action Planned by State against Stream Polluters." 18 October 1945. *Charleroi Mail*. Retrieved from http://search.ancestry.com/.

145 Dietrich, E.A. 1950. The Schuylkill Flows Green Again. *Pennsylvania Angler*, 19(2): 4-5. Retrieved from http://fishandboat.com/PaAnglerLegacyIssues.htm.

146 Hills, J.M. 1931. *River Coals of Eastern Pennsylvania. Bulletin No. 103*. Commonwealth of Pennsylvania, Department of Internal Affairs, Topographic and Geologic Survey. Retrieved from http://www.libraries.psu.edu/content/dam/psul/up/emsl/documents/pags_reports/no.103.pdf.

147 Webbert. 1920. *op. cit*

148 *Ibid.*

149 "Culm Stored For Icy Roads: State Turns To River After Severe Weather Cuts Cinder Supplies." 2 February 1948. *Reading Eagle.* Retrieved from http://news.google.com.

150 "Pennsylvania's Antipollution Progress: Bridgeport Ordered to Install Plant for Sewage Treatment" 1949. *Pennsylvania Angler,* 18(2): 25. Retrieved from http://fishandboat.com/PaAnglerLegacyIssues.htm.

151 Webbert. 1920. *op. cit.*

152 Water Supply Commission of Pennsylvania. 1916. *op. cit.*

153 U.S. Army. 1920. *Report of the Chief of Engineers, Part I.* Washington, D.C.: Government Printing Office. Retrieved from http://books.google.com/.

154 Kramer, H. 1928. *Study of the Culm Pollution Problem in the Schuylkill River, Pennsylvania.* Thesis, University of Pennsylvania. Philadelphia.

155 *Schuylkill River, Pa: Letter from the Secretary of War Transmitting a Letter from the Chief of Engineers, United States Army, Dated May 7, 1946, Submitting a Report, Together with Accompanying Papers and Illustrations, on a Preliminary Examination and Survey of and a Review of Reports on the Schuylkill River, Pa., Authorized by the River and Harbor Act Approved on March 2, 1945 and Also Requested by a Resolution of the Committee on Rivers and Harbors, House of Representatives, Adopted on March 8, 1945.* 1946. H.R.Doc. No. 699, 79th Cong., 2nd Session.

156 "Tragic Story of Sluggish Schuylkill to Be Written for Uncle Sam by Engineers Who Propose $10,000,000 'Bath' for River." 8 December 1935. *Reading Eagle.* Retrieved from http://news.google.com/.

157 *Schuylkill River, Pa: Letter from the Secretary of War Transmitting a Letter from the Chief of Engineers, United States Army, Dated May 7, 1946, Submitting a Report, Together with Accompanying Papers and Illustrations, on a Preliminary Examination and Survey of and a Review of Reports on the Schuylkill River, Pa., Authorized by the River and Harbor Act Approved on March 2, 1945 and Also Requested by a Resolution of the Committee on Rivers and Harbors, House of Representatives, Adopted on March 8, 1945.* 1946. H.R.Doc. No. 699, 79th Cong., 2nd Session.

158 Kramer. 1928. *op. cit.*

159 Biographical Publishing Company. 1898. *Book of Biography: Berks County, PA.* Buffalo, NY: Biographical Publishing Company.

160 "Government Survey of River Pollution May Start in Spring." 19 February 1927. *Reading Eagle.* Retrieved from http://news.google.com/.

161 "River Survey Given Impetus by Conference: Data Already On Hand

to Facilitate Solution of Culm Problem." 22 March 1927. *Reading Eagle.* Retrieved from http://news.google.com/.

162 "Tragic Story of Sluggish Schuylkill to Be Written for Uncle Sam by Engineers Who Propose $10,000,000 'Bath' for River." 8 December 1935. *Reading Eagle.* Retrieved from http://news.google.com/.

163 "River Survey May Be Halted: Funds Nearly Exhausted as Additional Sum Is Held Up." 1 October 1936. *Reading Eagle.* Retrieved from http://news.google.com/.

164 "Schuylkill Culm Deposits Studied." 1 January 1937. *Reading Eagle.* Retrieved from http://news.google.com/.

165 "City Favors River Plan." 8 July 1937. *Reading Eagle.* Retrieved from http://news.google.com/.

166 "River Survey May Be Halted: Funds Nearly Exhausted as Additional Sum Is Held Up." 1 October 1936. *Reading Eagle.* Retrieved from http://news.google.com/.

167 "Schuylkill River Project Opposed. Army Engineer Against Culm Removal." 15 November 1937. *Reading Eagle.* Retrieved from http://news.google.com/.

168 "River Report Is Assailed: Muhlenberg and Officials of State Seek U.S. Aid in Cleaning Schuylkill." 8 February 1938. *Reading Eagle.* Retrieved from http://news.google.com/.

169 Albert, R.C. 1988. The Historical Context of Water Quality Management for the Delaware Estuary. *Estuaries.* 11(2): 99-107.

170 Interstate Commission on the Delaware River Basin. 1945. *INCODEL: A Report on Its Activities and Accomplishments, July 1, 1943 to June 30, 1944.* Philadelphia, PA. Retrieved from http://lib.colostate.edu/archives/findingaids/water/wram.html.

171 An intercepting desilting basin was first proposed by the U.S. Army Corps of Engineers in 1939.

172 Ladner, G.C. 1944. "Schuylkill River Clean-Up in Sight." *Pennsylvania Park News*, No. 39 September, 1944. Retrieved from http://archive.org/.

173 "Post War Labor to Clean Streams." 15 December 1944. *Pittsburgh Press.* Retrieved from http://news.google.com/.

174 *Schuylkill River, Pa: Letter from the Secretary of War Transmitting a Letter from the Chief of Engineers, United States Army, Dated May 7, 1946, Submitting a Report, Together with Accompanying Papers and Illustrations, on a Preliminary Examination and Survey of and a Review of Reports on the Schuylkill River, Pa., Authorized by the River and Harbor Act Approved on March 2, 1945 and Also Requested by a Resolution of the Committee on Rivers and Harbors, House of Representatives, Adopted on March 8, 1945.*

1946. H.R.Doc. No. 699, 79th Cong., 2nd Session.

175 Schuylkill River Project Engineers. 1951. *op. cit.*

176 Wolf. 1949. *op cit.*

The Worst First

177 "Positive Desilting Plan Urged for Schuylkill." 6 March 1947. *Pottstown Mercury.* Retrieved from http://search.ancestry.com/.

178 Schuylkill River Project Engineers. 1951. *op. cit.*

179 Wolf. 1949. *op. cit.*

180 U.S. Patent Office. 1934. 1966886, Water Gas Process. Retrieved from www.google.com/patents/US1966886.pdf.

181 "Friel, Prominent Engineer Dies." 13 February 1964. *Delaware County Daily Times.* Retrieved from http://search.ancestry.com.

182 University of Chicago Alumni Association. 1917. *The University of Chicago Magazine*, 10(1): 194. University of Chicago Alumni Council. Retrieved from http://books.google.com/.

183 Schuylkill River Project Engineers. 1951. *op. cit.*

184 Dechant, F.H. *Letter to M.F. Draemel.* 12 March 1947. Schuylkill River Archival Collection, Montgomery County Community College, Blue Bell, PA.

185 "Pennsylvania's Anti-Pollution Progress: Schuylkill Will Show Improvement Through Desilting Drive." 1948. *Pennsylvania Angler,* 17(9): 25. Retrieved from http://fishandboat.com/PaAnglerLegacyIssues.htm.

186 Commonwealth of Pennsylvania. 1948. *The Schuylkill River Project: Restoring a Natural Resource to the People of Pennsylvania.* Harrisburg, PA.

187 Nolan, J.B. 2004. *The Schuylkill.* New Brunswick, NJ: Rutgers University Press. Original published 1951.

188 U.S. Bureau of Labor Statistics. n.d. *CPI Inflation Calculator.* Retrieved from http://www.bls.gov/data/inflation_calculator.htm.

189 Draemel, M.F. 11 September 1949. *Memo to M.A. Laverty.* Schuylkill River Archival Collection, Montgomery County Community College, Blue Bell, PA.

190 Sword, S.H. 7 January 1955. *Letter to R.J. Gillis.* Schuylkill River Archival Collection, Montgomery County Community College, Blue Bell, PA.

191 Schuylkill River Project Engineers. *op cit.*

192 Some contractors also acted as subcontractors to other contractors. Not

all subcontractors may be listed in the *Final Report of the Schuylkill River Project Engineers.*

193 "5 Schuylkill Dams to Be Torn Down." 30 October 1947. *Pottstown Mercury.* Retrieved from http://search.ancestry.com/.

194 In the years since the Schuylkill River Project, the terms "impounding basin" and "desilting basin" have become interchangeable for many speaking about the structures. The Schuylkill River Project Engineers used the term impounding basin to refer to the areas created to receive dredge spoils. The term desilting basin referred to the pools resulting from the construction of dams at Auburn, Kernsville, and Tamaqua designed to catch future coal silt moving downstream.

195 Schuylkill River Project Engineers. 1951. *op. cit.*

196 *Ibid.*

197 A water year begins on October 1st of a given year and runs through September 30th of the following year.

198 Commonwealth of Pennsylvania in cooperation with the U.S. Department of Interior–Geological Survey. 1950. *Water Resource Investigations Relating to the Schuylkill River Restoration Project.* Harrisburg, PA.

199 Schuylkill River Project Engineers. 1951. *op. cit.*

200 "River Work Pollutes Wells at Neversink." 2 February 1950. *Reading Eagle.* Retrieved from http://news.google.com/.

201 Schuylkill River Project Engineers. 1951. *op. cit.*

202 U.S. Bureau of Labor Statistics. n.d. *op. cit.*

203 "Debris Hinders Dredge Work on Schuylkill." 15 November 1949. *Reading Eagle.* Retrieved from http://news.google.com/.

204 Schuylkill River Project Engineers. 1951. *op. cit.*

205 Commonwealth of Pennsylvania in cooperation with the U.S. Department of Interior–Geological Survey. 1950. *op. cit.*

206 Schmidt, F.J. 1950. Portable Dredged Split 3 Ways to Fit Through Schuylkill River Locks. *Engineering News-Record*, 143(17): 38-39. Albany, NY: McGraw-Hill Publishing Co., Inc.

207 *Ibid.*

208 *Ibid.*

209 Commonwealth of Pennsylvania in cooperation with the U.S. Department of Interior–Geological Survey. 1950. *op. cit.*

210 Schmidt. 1950. *op. cit.*

211 Commonwealth of Pennsylvania in cooperation with the U.S.

Department of Interior–Geological Survey. 1950. *op. cit.*

212 *Ibid.*

213 U.S. Bureau of Labor Statistics. n.d. *op. cit.*

214 *Ibid.*

215 Schuylkill River Project Engineers. 1951. *op. cit.*

216 Zisman, S.B. 1949. *Report #1: The Schuylkill River Project.* Citizens' Council on City Planning. Unpublished.

217 Schuylkill River Project Engineers. 1951. *op. cit.*

218 *Ibid.*

219 *Ibid.*

220 "Two Docks Will Aid Future Silt Removal: Dredge placed in 'Mothballs' in Kernsville; Original Schuylkill Project May End in June." 28 February 1951. *Reading Eagle.* Retrieved from http://news.google.com/.

221 Commonwealth of Pennsylvania. 1985. *Schuylkill River Project Desilting Pools and Impounding Basins.* Harrisburg, PA.

222 Schuylkill River Project Engineers. 1951. *op. cit.*

223 *Ibid.*

224 *Ibid.*

225 Vaux, N. 1949. The Farmer and Pollution. *Pennsylvania Angler,* 18(8): 4, 16. Retrieved from http://fishandboat.com/PaAnglerLegacyIssues.htm.

226 Schuylkill River Project Engineers. 1951. *op. cit.*

227 *Ibid.*

228 "Pennsylvania Cleans its Worst River" *Engineering News-Record,* 142(10): 21-24. Albany, NY: McGraw-Hill Publishing Co., Inc.

229 Commonwealth of Pennsylvania. 1985. *op. cit.*

230 Schuylkill River Project Engineers. 1951. *op. cit.*

231 Commonwealth of Pennsylvania. 1985. *op. cit.*

232 Schuylkill River Project Engineers. 1951. *op. cit.*

233 *Ibid.*

234 Commonwealth of Pennsylvania. 1985. *op. cit.*

235 *Ibid.*

236 Biesecker. 1968. *op. cit.*

237 Not all coal wastes discharges were being prevented. The Sanitary Water Board ordered mining companies to construct their own silt trapping basin. The *Final Report of the Schuylkill River Project Engineers* noted that

discharges from these basins contained "not more than 1000 parts per million of suspended solids." (Schuylkill River Project Engineers, 1951). Current Pennsylvania regulations require that suspended solids in the effluent from coal mining operations average less than 35 milligrams per liter over 30 days (§87.102. Hydrologic balance: effluent standards).

238 Sanitary Water Board. 1949. Schuylkill Cleanup Greatest Accomplishment of Its Kind. *Clean Streams,* March, No .8. Harrisburg, PA: Pennsylvania Department of Health.

239 "Deadline Set To End River Pollution." 19 December 1948. *Reading Eagle*. Retrieved from http://news.google.com/.

240 Commonwealth of Pennsylvania. 1985. *op. cit.*

241 Total costs were less than the $35 million appropriated.

242 U.S. Bureau of Labor Statistics. n.d. *op. cit.*

243 Stirling, P. 1955. Rebirth of a River. *The Military Engineer*, 47(316) 119-120.

244 *Ibid.*

245 "Millions of Birds To Have City Feeding Place Saved." 21 August 1953. *Indiana Evening Gazette*. Retrieved from http://search.ancestry.com/.

246 *Ibid.*

247 Natural Lands Trust. 2012. *Mission and History*. Retrieved from http://www.natlands.org/who-we-are/mission-and-history/

248 "Millions of Birds To Have City Feeding Place Saved." 21 August 1953. *Indiana Evening Gazette*. Retrieved from http://search.ancestry.com/.

249 Commonwealth of Pennsylvania. 1985. *op. cit.*

250 Stirling. 1955. *op. cit.*

251 "Eastwick, Philadelphia, Pennsylvania." 23 May 2012. *Wikipedia*. Retrieved from http://en.wikipedia.org/wiki/Eastwick,_Philadelphia,_Pennsylvania

252 Melamed, S. 26 April 2012. "Sinking Feeling." *City Paper*. Retrieved from http://www.citypaper.net/news/2012-04-26-sinking-houses-north-philly-land.html?c=r

253 "Job of Freeing the Susquehanna Now Progressed To Tribs. Swatara Creek Freed of Coal Silt: Results compared to Schuylkill Project." 9 January 1949. *Reading Eagle*. Retrieved from http://news.google.com/.

254 "Propose Desilting Basin for Cuyahoga River." 1949. *Engineering News-Record*, 142(10) 21-24. Albany, NY: McGraw-Hill Publishing Co., Inc.

255 Rosendale, R.L. 2 April 1951. *Draft Letter to E.J. Fitzmaurice*. Rosendale

Papers. In possession of the author, Bristol, PA.

Working on the Schuylkill River Project

256 Schuylkill River Project Engineers. 1951. *op. cit.*

257 "River Cleanup First of Many, Duff Asserts." 1948. Unidentified newspaper clipping. Rosendale Papers. In possession of the author, Bristol, PA.

258 "Chief of Schuylkill Survey Gets Leave." 22 April 1946. *Reading Eagle.* Retrieved from http://news.google.com/.

259 Schuylkill River Project Engineers. 4 April 1950. *Disposition of Forces – Construction Division.* Unpublished. In possession of the author, Bristol, PA.

260 Schuylkill River Project Engineers. 30 September 1948. *Field Inventory at Riverside Disposal Area.* Unpublished. In possession of the author, Bristol, PA.

261 A shifter is a small engine used in a switching yard to assemble cars in a train.

262 Schuylkill River Project Engineers. 1951. *op. cit.*

263 "State Pushes Holiday Clean-up: Local Crews To Receive Brief Rest." 20 December 1949. *Reading Eagle.* Retrieved from http://news.google.com/.

264 "Dredge Tamaqua Now in Operation at Desilting Dam." 21 February 1951. *Tamaqua Evening Courier.*

265 Sword, S.H. 7 November 1955. *Letter to W. E. Kirkpatrick.* Schuylkill River Archival Collection, Montgomery County Community College, Blue Bell, PA.

266 Farquhar, M. et al. 1996. *Private Land Mobile Radio Services: Background.* Federal Communications Commission, Wireless Telecommunications Bureau. Retrieved from http://wireless.fcc.gov/reports/documents/whtepapr.pdf.

267 Pennsylvania Department of Environmental Protection. n.d. *History: A Chronology of Events in Pennsylvania Forestry Showing Things As They Happened to Penn's Woods.* Retrieved from http://www.portal.state.pa.us/portal/server.pt?open=514&objID=588459&mode=2.

268 *Ibid.*

269 Schuylkill River Project Engineers. 1951. *op. cit.*

270 "Debris Hinders Dredge Work on Schuylkill. "15 November 1949. *Reading Eagle.* Retrieved from http://news.google.com/.

271 Eel weirs are long stone or wood structures that extend out into the river to form a "V" shape with the tip pointed downstream. The adult

eels would be caught in a trap at the tip of the "V" as they migrated downstream.

272 Stirling. 1955. *op. cit.*

273 "River Work Pollutes Wells at Neversink." 2 February 1950. *Reading Eagle.* Retrieved from http://news.google.com/.

274 Stirling, P. 1955. *op. cit.*

275 Unidentified newspaper clipping. Rosendale Papers. Original in possession of the author, Bristol, PA.

276 "Water Begins Flowing Over Kernsville Dam." 3 September 1949. *Reading Eagle.* Retrieved from http://news.google.com/.

277 "N.Y Firm Files Appeal: Case of Damaged Tractor Carried to State Supreme Court." 30 November 1954. *Reading Eagle.* Retrieved from http://news.google.com/.

278 Mowrer v. Poirier & McLane Corp, 382 Pa. 2 (1955).

279 "Truck Kills 2 Working on Schuylkill River Job." 3 June 1950. *Reading Times.*

280 "Survey for New Source of Water Considered by Borough Committee." 31 October 1947. *Pottstown Mercury.* Retrieved from http://search.ancestry.com/.

281 Vaux, N. 1949. *op. cit.*

Selling Silt

282 In 1935, Pennsylvania formed the General State Authority, an independent public corporation, that allowed the Commonwealth to bypass constitutional restrictions on borrowing money. The 1935 General State Authority was abolished in 1945, but with Duff's aggressive building program, a new General State Authority was created in 1949. This agency existed until 1975 when it was merged with the Department of Property and Supplies to form the Department of General Services.

283 The final total cost of the original Schuylkill River Project was $31,784,744.11.

284 Schoffstall, M. 9 August 1948. "River Coal May Slash Schuylkill Cleanup Costs." *Reading Times.*

285 "Arrow Is Shot Across Schuylkill In Plan to Replace Dredge Cable." 15 November 1947. *Reading Eagle.* Retrieved from http://news.google.com/.

286 "End of Dredging To Boost Coal Bill." 20 December 1948. *Reading Eagle.* Retrieved from http://news.google.com/.

287 *Ibid.*

288 Biesecker. 1968. *op. cit.*

289 "State Picks Sites To Store River Culm: Dredging Operations in Schuylkill Will Be Next Phase of Cleaning Project." 24 February 1948. *Reading Eagle.* Retrieved from http://news.google.com/.

290 "The Construction Week." 1948. *Engineering News-Record,* 141(23): 3. Albany, NY: McGraw-Hill Publishing Co., Inc.

291 "$50,000 in Coal Dirt Damages for Farmers." 16 May 1901. *Reading Eagle.* Retrieved from http://news.google.com/

292 "Refuse of River Coal Hurt Farm." 30 November 1961. *Reading Eagle.* Retrieved from http://news.google.com/

293 "Coal Dirt Replaces Cinders on Icy Roads." 2 February 1948. *Reading Eagle.* Retrieved from http://news.google.com/.

294 Schoffstall. 1948. *op .cit.*

295 "Halloween Fete Planned: West Reading Trade Board Hears Review of Borough Activities." 12 October 1949. *Reading Eagle.* Retrieved from http://news.google.com/.

296 "West Reading Council Calls Conference on Smoke and Soot." 7 September 1949. *Reading Eagle.* Retrieved from http://news.google.com/.

297 "State Received No Bids for River Culm." 3 January 1951. *Reading Eagle.* Retrieved from http://news.google.com/.

298 "Mahanoy Firm Bids on Coal Silt." 21 June 1951. *Reading Eagle.* Retrieved from http://news.google.com/.

299 Guertler, E. 2011. "Schuylkill Haven Historical Society: Charles D. Manbeck - A Horatio Alger Man." *Haven Highlights,* No. 28, 23-27. Retrieved from http://southschuylkill.net/yahoo_site_admin/assets/docs/Haven_Newsletter.37110104.pdf.

300 Geier, I. 12 January 1974. " 'Firsts' Pepper Coal Entrepreneur's Life: Manbeck Trailblazed With Trucks, 'Coolerator,' More." *Pottsville Republican.* Reprinted in "Eight By Ione." n.d. Retrieved from http://www.schuylkill.com/pub/archive/ione/ione3.htm.

301 "Culm Yields Revenue for Pennsylvania." 18 May 1952. *Reading Eagle.* Retrieved from http://news.google.com/.

302 *Ibid.*

303 *Ibid.*

304 "One Bid Received for River Waste." 21 May 1965. *Reading Eagle.* Retrieved from http://news.google.com/.

305 Biesecker. 1968. *op. cit.*

306 Commonwealth of Pennsylvania. 1985. *op. cit.*

307 Patrick, R. 1949. "A Proposed Biological Measure of Stream Conditions, Based on a Survey of the Conestoga Basin, Lancaster County, Pennsylvania." *Proceedings of the Academy of Natural Sciences of Philadelphia*, Vol. 101, 277-341. Retrieved from http://www.jstor.org/stable/4064427.

Canaries of the Stream

308 Mine Safety and Health Administration. n.d. *Canaries. A Pictorial Walk Through the 20th Century.* Retrieved from http://www.msha.gov/century/canary/canary.asp.

309 BBC.com. n.d. 1986: Coal Mine Canaries Made Redundant. *On this Day 1950 – 2005.* Retrieved from http://news.bbc.co.uk/onthisday/hi/dates/stories/december/30/newsid_2547000/2547587.stm.

310 Patrick. 1949. *op. cit.*

311 Distinguished Daughters of Pennsylvania. 2008. *60th Anniversary Directory of the Distinguished Daughters of Pennsylvania.* Retrieved from http://distinguisheddaughtersofpa.files.wordpress.com/2011/10/1949-to-2008-directory.pdf.

312 John Cairns wishes to acknowledge Darla Donald for transcribing the handwritten draft and for editorial assistance in preparation for publication.

313 "Science Plays Important Role in Pennsylvania Stream Clearance." 1948. *Pennsylvania Angler*, 17(10): 12-13. Retrieved from http://fishandboat.com/PaAnglerLegacyIssues.htm.

314 U.S. Environmental Protection Agency. 1991. *Policy on the Use of Biological Assessments and Criteria in the Water Quality Program.* U.S. Environmental Protection Agency, Washington, DC. Retrieved from http://www.epa.gov/bioiweb1/pdf/PolicyonBiologicalAssessmentsandCriteria.pdf.

315 Dolan, T, IV. 18 June 2012. *Memo to C. Towne.* In possession of the author, Bristol, PA.

316 Commonwealth of Pennsylvania in cooperation with the U.S. Department of Interior–Geological Survey. 1950. *op. cit.*

317 *Ibid.*

318 *Ibid.*

319 *Ibid.*

320 Biesecker. 1968. *op. cit.*

321 Duff, J.H. 1945. Stream Pollution. *Pennsylvania Angler*, 9(2): 2, 3, 16. Retrieved from http://fishandboat.com/PaAnglerLegacyIssues.htm.

The River Endures

322 Wohl, E., et al. 2004. *CUAHSI Vision Paper on River Restoration.* Fall 2004 Vision Paper Cyberseminar Series. Consortium of Universities for the Advancement of Hydrologic Science, Inc. Retrieved from http://www.cuahsi.org/cyberseminars/Wohl-20040923.pdf.

323 Duff. 1945. *op. cit.*

324 *Ibid.*

325 P.L. 1383, No. 441 of 1945.

326 "Lessons in Forestry." 18 September 1885. *New York Times.* Retrieved from http://www.nytimes.com/ref/membercenter/nytarchive.html.

327 Ludlow. 1885. *op. cit.*

328 *Ibid.*

329 Run-of-the-river dams can actually make flooding worse by eliminating storage capacity in the floodplain that would have been available had the dam not been present. The presence of a run-of-the-river dam can also make flooding worse upstream of the structure and impoundment by keeping the river in a bankfull condition at all times.

330 Poff, L.N. and Hart, D.D. 2002. How Dams Vary and Why It Matters for the Emerging Science of Dam Removal. *BioScience.*, 52(8): 661-667

331 *Report of the President and Managers of the Schuylkill Navigation Company to Stockholders.* 1836. Philadelphia: James Kay, Jr., and Brother. Retrieved from http://books.google.com.

332 Ellet, C., Jr. 1847. Schuylkill Navigation Company. *American Railroad Journal and General Advertiser.* Second Quarto Series 3(37): 16, Whole no. 586(20): 582-585. Philadelphia. Retrieved from http://archive.org/.

333 *Report of the President and Managers of the Schuylkill Navigation Company to Stockholders.* 1854. Philadelphia: Crissey and Markley. Retrieved from http://books.google.com.

334 U.S. Army. 1922. *Annual Report of the Chief of Engineers.* Washington, D.C.: Government Printing Office.

335 Schuylkill River Project Engineers. 1951. *op. cit.*

336 Biesecker. 1968. *op. cit.*

337 Webbert. 1920. *op. cit.*

338 Biesecker. 1968. *op. cit.*

339 "The Construction Week." 1948. *Engineering News-Record,* 141(23): 3. Albany, NY: McGraw-Hill Publishing Co., Inc.

340 Pitkin, F.A. 1944. Game Lands in State Planning Program. *Forest Leaves.* 34(2): 1-2.Narbeth, PA: Pennsylvania Forestry Association. Retrieved

from http://archive.org/.

341 Degnan, M.E., et al. 2007. *Sediment Quality Of The Schuylkill River: A Cooperative USGS, PWD, and WCU Study.* Paper presented at the Geological Society of America Annual Meeting. Retrieved from https://gsa.confex.com/gsa/2007AM/finalprogram/abstract_131962.htm.

342 Schuylkill River Project Engineers. 1951. *op. cit.*

343 Biesecker. 1968. *op. cit.*

344 "Schuylkill Project Hit: Draemel Defends Operation as Aid To Flood Control." 27 March 1951. *Reading Eagle.* Retrieved from http://news.google.com/.

345 Schuylkill River Project Engineers. 1951. *op. cit.*

346 *Ibid.*

347 Black, W.A. 11 August 1948. *Memo to Accounting Department.* Rosendale Papers. In possession of the author, Bristol, PA.

348 "River Project Fails to Cut Flood Damages." 31 December 1948. *Reading Eagle.* Retrieved from http://news.google.com/.

349 Schuylkill River Project Engineers. 1951. *op. cit.*

350 "Storm Sends Schuylkill to Flood Stage." 22 November 1952. *Reading Eagle.* Retrieved from http://news.google.com/.

351 "Dredging Criticized As Flood Retarder." 28 August 1955. *New York Times.* Retrieved from http://query.nytimes.com/mem/archive/pdf?res=F70817FF3555127B93CAAB1783D85F418585F9.

352 *Ibid.*

353 Chesapeake Bay Foundation. 1998. *A Dollars and Sense Partnership: Economic Development and Environmental Protection.*

354 Delaware Department of Natural Resources Environmental Control and Brandywine Conservancy. 1997. *Conservation Design for Stormwater Management: A Design Approach to Reduce Stormwater Impacts from Land Development and Achieve Multiple Objectives Related to Land Use.*

355 Podniesinski, G. et al. 2005. *Vegetation Classification and Mapping of Valley Forge National Historical Park. Technical Report NPS/NER/NRTR—2005/028.* National Park Service. Philadelphia, PA. Retrieved from http://www.nps.gov/nero/science/FINAL/VAFO_vegmap/VAFO_vegmap_1.pdf.

356 Moses, T. 2012. *The Schuylkill River Flood Control Project – One Restoration Practitioner's Perspective.* Unpublished.

357 *Ibid.*

358 "Port Clinton Tunnel Abandoned and Course of Schuylkill Changed by Reading Co. at that Point." 17 May 1926. *Reading Eagle.* Retrieved from

http://news.google.com/

359 Schuylkill River Project Engineers. 1951. *op. cit.*

360 Chubb, R.S. and Merkel, P.P. 1946. Effect of Acid Wastes on Natural Purification of the Schuylkill River. *Sewage Works Journal*, 18(4): 692-694. Water Environment Federation. Retrieved from: http://www.jstor.org/stable/25030291.

Acid to Reading

361 International News Service. 14 January 1949. "Capital Whirl." *The Connellsville Daily Courier.* Retrieved from http://search.ancestry.com/.

362 International News Service. 6 May 1950. "Capital Whirl." *The Connellsville Daily Courier.* Retrieved from http://search.ancestry.com/.

363 "Governor Duff Promises Schuylkill Cleanup." 2 May 1947. *Pottstown Mercury.* Retrieved from http://search.ancestry.com/.

364 "Fine Budget Calls For Higher Taxes To Pay State's Obligation." 20 March 1951. *Jeannette News Dispatch.* Retrieved from http://news.google.com/.

365 "Schuylkill River Cleanup Costs Said Below Estimate." 6 October 1950. *Lebanon Daily News.* Retrieved from http://search.ancestry.com/.

366 "$25,000 Property Leased By PA, To Ex-Owner For $1." 27 March 1951. *Tyrone Daily Herald.* Retrieved from http://search.ancestry.com/.

367 "Harmony Rules As Duff Begins Governorship." 22 January 1947. *Pittsburgh Press.* Retrieved from http://news.google.com/.

368 "Gasoline, Soft Drink Levies Pass Senate." 16 March 1949. *Washington Reporter.* Retrieved from http://news.google.com/.

369 "Dent Protests Turnpike Food: Senator Complains of 'Exorbitant' Prices Charged." 9 September 1947. *Greeensburg Daily Tribune.* Retrieved from http://news.google.com/.

370 "State to Check Materials Taken from Schuylkill." 26 October 1955. *Monessen Daily Independent.* Retrieved from http://search.ancestry.com/.

371 "Paul Sanger Hits Duff's Desire To Rebuild GOP." 18 November 1954. *Lebanon Daily News.* Retrieved from http://search.ancestry.com/.

372 "Clean Stream Progress in State Told." 13 November 1952. *Indiana Evening Gazette.* Retrieved from http://search.ancestry.com/.

373 *Ibid.*

374 "Keystone State's Vast Stream Clearance Program Being Carried Out Over Wide Front at High Cost." 18 November 1950. *Connellsville Daily Courier.* Retrieved from http://search.ancestry.com/.

375 "Sewage Flow Into Schuylkill Halted Today." 7 May 1951. *Reading Eagle*. Retrieved from http://news.google.com/.

376 Schuylkill River Project Engineers. 1951. *op. cit.*

377 Pipeline for Sewerage at Reading, PA. 26 October 1895. *Scientific American*, 73(17): 268. New York: Munn & Co. Retrieved from http://books.google.com/.

378 "Schuylkill Showing Signs of Revival Here." 24 May 1948. *Reading Eagle*.

379 Hazen and Whipple, Consulting & Civil Engineers. 29 February 1912. "Pittsburgh Sewage Disposal Reports." *Engineering News*, 67(9): 398-402. New York: Hill Publishing Company.

380 "R.S. Chubb Dies at 58: Retired City Engineer Stricken While on Visit." 13 February 1958. *Reading Eagle*. Retrieved from http://news.google.com/.

381 Chubb, R.S. 12 March 1945. *Letter to Honorable James H. Duff.* Pennsylvania State Archives. Pennsylvania Historic and Museums Commission.

382 Chubb and Merkel. 1946. *op. cit.*

383 Biesecker. 1968. *op. cit.*

384 U.S. Geological Survey. 9 March 2012. A million gallons of water—How much is it? *Water Science for Schools*. Retrieved from http://ga.water.usgs.gov/edu/mgd.html.

385 P.L. 372, No. 194 of 1965.

386 Biesecker. 1968. *op. cit.*

387 "Schuylkill Project Hit: Draemel Defends Operation as Aid To Flood Control." 27 March 1951. *Reading Eagle*. Retrieved from http://news.google.com/.

388 "Martin to Act on Most PA. Measures Today." 4 June 1945. *Clearfield Progress*. Retrieved from http://search.ancestry.com/.

389 "Postwar Building Program Is Well Advanced in State." 7 June 1945. *Charleroi Mail*. Retrieved from http://search.ancestry.com/.

390 Dietrich. 1950. *op. cit.*

Breaking with the Past

391 "Survey for New Source of Water Considered by Borough Committee." 31 October 1947. *Pottstown Mercury*. Retrieved from http://search.ancestry.com/.

392 "At Last a Move for a Better Water Supply." 26 February 1945. *Philadelphia Inquirer*. Retrieved from http://www.phillyh2o.org/backpages/PWDNewsClips1944to46.pdf.

393 "Objection Filed By Lehigh Company to City Water Plan." 12 December 1945. *Philadelphia Record*. Retrieved from http://www.phillyh2o.org/backpages/PWDNewsClips1944to46.pdf.

394 P.L. 1383, No. 441 of 1945.

395 Mock. 1944. *op. cit.*

396 "Upland Water Supply Plans Shelved By Official Report: Action First on Bettering Local Source." 12 November 1946. *Philadelphia Evening Bulletin*. Retrieved from http://www.phillyh2o.org/backpages/PWDNewsClips1944to46.pdf.

397 "Conservation Is Vital, Duff Asserts Here." 18 October 1948. *Uniontown Morning Herald*. Retrieved from http://search.ancestry.com/.

398 *Ibid.*

399 Commonwealth of Pennsylvania in cooperation with the U.S. Department of Interior–Geological Survey. 1950. *op. cit.*

400 Biesecker. 1968. *op. cit.*

401 "Action Planned By State Against Stream Polluters." 18 October 1945. *Charleroi Mail*. Retrieved from http://search.ancestry.com/.

402 Ash, S.H., et al. 1951. *Acid Mine Drainage Problems. Anthracite Region of Pennsylvania. Bulletin 508*. Department of Interior, Bureau of Mines. Washington, D.C.: Government Printing Office.

403 "State To Dredge Felix Dam Area: Goddard Reported Cool To Schuylkill Park Plan." 5 March 1957. *Reading Eagle*. Retrieved from http://news.google.com/.

404 "Pottsville Refused Federal Grant." 29 November 1958. *Reading Eagle*. Retrieved from http://news.google.com/.

405 "State Cites Municipalities on Pollution." 23 October 1968. *Washington Observer-Reporter*. Retrieved from http://news.google.com/.

406 Wildcat sewers remain a problem in other parts of Pennsylvania as well. In 2006, the number of homes in southwestern Pennsylvania with wildcat sewers was estimated at 27,000 by the Regional Water Management Task Force in *Regional Water Management in Southwestern Pennsylvania: Moving Toward a Solution*, http://www.iop.pitt.edu/water/RWMTF%20Framing%20Paper.pdf.

407 Plasko, J. 25 November 2009. "Schuylkill Valley Sewer Authority receives EPA Pisces Award." *Times News*. Retrieved from http://www.tnonline.com/2009/nov/25/schuylkill-valley-sewer-authority-receives-epa-pisces-award.

408 "Women and Girls at Work Digging Sewers." 4 August 1932. *Reading Eagle*. Retrieved from http://news.google.com/.

409 Pinkey, L. "54 Wildcat Sewers Still Unconnected" 7 September 2011. *Times News.* Retrieved from http://www.tnonline.com/2011/sep/07/54-wildcat-sewers-still-unconnected.

410 "Tamaqua Voters Defeat Ballot Question on Sewers" 9 November 2011. *Times News.* Retrieved from http://www.tnonline.com/2011/nov/09/tamaqua-voters-defeat-ballot-question-sewers.

411 Spatz, D. 16 February 2012. "Reading Looking at Cheaper Fix for Fritz's Island Sewage Plant." *Reading Eagle.* Retrieved from http://readingeagle.com/article.aspx?id=287905.

412 Workshop of the World—Philadelphia. 2007. Fairmount Park: Belmont Petroleum Refinery. *Workshop of the World—Philadelphia.* Retrieved from http://www.workshopoftheworld.com/fairmount_park/belmont_petroleum.html.

413 "The River Set on Fire." 2 November 1892. *New York Times.* Retrieved from http://www.nytimes.com/ref/membercenter/nytarchive.html.

414 Kernan v. American Dredging Co., 355 U.S. 426 (1958).

415 Leidy, J. 1884. Urnatella Gracilus, A Fresh Water Protozoan. *Journal of the Academy of Natural Sciences of Philadelphia*, 10(2): 5-16. Philadelphia: Kildare's Printing House. Retrieved from http://books.google.com/.

416 U.S. Environmental Protection Agency. 28 March 2012. *Sunoco, Inc. - Point Breeze.* Retrieved from http://www.epa.gov/reg3wcmd/ca/pa/webpages/pad002289700.html.

417 "Guard Oil Slick on Schuylkill." 7 December 1953. *Gettysburg Times.* Retrieved from http://news.google.com/.

418 The 1989 "Exxon Valdez" oil spill, to that date the largest oil spill in U.S. history, dumped over 11 million gallons of crude oil into Prince William Sound.

419 Altenburg, Kirk and Company. Inc. 1970. *Oil on the Schuylkill: A Case Study.* U.S. Environmental Protection Agency.

420 Duff. 1945. *op. cit.*

421 "Conservation of Soil Is Stressed By Governor." 22 October 1947. *Coatesville Record.* Reprinted in *Conservation of Soil, Governor James Duff.* Special Collections of West Chester University.

422 Wolman, M.G. 1972. The Nation's Rivers. *Journal of the Water Pollution Control Federation*, 44(5): 715-737. Water Environment Federation. Retrieved from http://www.jstor.org/stable/25037448.

423 "Three Berks Farmers Sue 21 Coal Operators." 11 September 1899. *Reading Eagle.* Retrieved from http://news.google.com/.

424 *Pennsylvania Coal Co. v. Sanderson*, 113 Pa. 126, 1886.

425 Pitkin. 1944. *op. cit.*

426 "A Lesson in Forestry." 18 September 1885. *New York Times*. Retrieved from http://www.nytimes.com/ref/membercenter/nytarchive.html.

427 Wolman. 1972. *op. cit.*

428 Biesecker. 1968. *op. cit.*

429 Wolman. 1972. *op. cit.*

430 Mansue, L.J. and Cummings, A.B. 1974. *Sediment Transport By Streams Draining Into the Delaware Estuary. Hydrologic Effects of Land Use. Water Supply Paper 1532-H.* U.S, Geological Survey. Washington, D.C.: Government Printing Office. Retrieved from http://books.google.com/.

431 Barrows, H.K., et al. 1909. *Surface Water Supply of the United States. Part I. North Atlantic Coast. Water Supply Paper 261.* U.S. Geological Survey. Washington, D.C.: Government Printing Office. Retrieved from http://books.google.com/.

432 Pennsylvania Department of Environmental Protection. 2012. *Draft 2012 Pennsylvania Integrated Water Quality Monitoring and Assessment Report - Streams, Category 5 Waterbodies, Pollutants Requiring a TMDL.* Retrieved from http://www.portal.state.pa.us/portal/server.pt/community/water_quality_standards/10556/integrated_water_quality_report_-_2012/1127203.

433 "Dredging Project Set: Cleanup of Felix Pool in Schuylkill Scheduled for Spring." 10 November 1959. *Reading Eagle*. Retrieved from http://news.google.com/.

434 Commonwealth of Pennsylvania. 1985. *op. cit.*

435 McCullough, J.G. 8 June 1952. "Cleanup Makes the Upper Schuylkill Glisten." *Philadelphia Sunday Bulletin*.

436 Early, J.R. "Dam Removal Urged to Cut Flood Hazard." 27 June 1943. *Reading Eagle*. Retrieved from http://news.google.com/.

437 "Schuylkill Showing Signs of Revival Here." 24 May 1948. *Reading Eagle*.

438 "Civic Group Organized to Fight For Schuylkill Dam Retention." 1 June 1949. *Reading Eagle*. Retrieved from http://news.google.com/.

439 "Schuylkill Showing Signs of Revival Here." 24 May 1948. *Reading Eagle*.

440 "No Recreation Plans Included In River Work, McCawley Says" 15 June 1949. *Reading Eagle*. Retrieved from http://news.google.com/.

441 Schuylkill River Project Engineers. 1951. *op. cit.*

442 Sword, S.H. 31 January 1955. 3 May 1960. *Letter to M.M. Mallon.* Schuylkill River Archival Collection, Montgomery County Community College, Blue Bell, PA.

443 DeMarte, P.J. 3 May 1960. *Memo to L. Cross.* Schuylkill River Archival Collection, Montgomery County Community College, Blue Bell, PA.

444 Sword, S.H. 13 April 1955. *Letter to H. King.* Schuylkill River Archival Collection, Montgomery County Community College, Blue Bell, PA.

445 Dodson, J.P. 30 August 1967. *Letter to J.C.E. Bouchard.* Schuylkill River Archival Collection, Montgomery County Community College, Blue Bell, PA.

446 Commonwealth of Pennsylvania. 1985. *op. cit.*

447 P.L. 1383, No. 441 of 1945.

448 Commonwealth of Pennsylvania. 1985. *op. cit.*

449 *Ibid.*

450 Whitemarsh Township. 2006. *Open Space Plan: Chapter 3.1 Existing Protected Lands.* Retrieved from http://www.whitemarshtwp.org/pdf/osp/chapter-3.1.pdf.

451 Pennsylvania Department of Conservation and Natural Resources. n.d. *Heuser Park, Upper Merion Township, Montgomery County, PA.* Retrieved from http://www.dcnr.state.pa.us/ucmprd1/groups/public/documents/document/d_001332.pdf.

452 Chester County. n.d. *Black Rock Sanctuary.* Retrieved from http://dsf.chesco.org/ccparks/cwp/view.asp?a=1550&q=616465.

453 Chester County's Facilities Management and Parks and Recreation departments were merged in 2010 creating the Facilities and Parks Department.

454 Montgomery County. 2012. *Schuylkill River Greenway.* Retrieved from http://openspaceprogram.montcopa.org/openspaceprogram/cwp/view.asp?a=1487&q=82300&openspaceprogramNav=|.

455 Salaneck, J. 5 August 2011. "Union Township expands recreation area with 2-mile trail." *Bctv.org.* Retrieved from http://www.bctv.org/special_reports/basic_needs/union-township-expands-recreation-area-with-mile-trail/article_6ecd099c-bf6d-11e0-a5e0-001cc4c03286.html.

456 In 1970, the Department of Environmental Resources was formed through the consolidation of 17 pollution control/resource management agencies, boards and commissions, including the Department of Forests and Waters. As a result the Department of Environmental Resources inherited the lands associated with the Schuylkill River Project. In 1995, when the Department of Environmental Resources was split into the Department of Environmental Protection and the Department of Conservation and Natural Resources, the remaining Schuylkill River Project lands stayed with the Department of Environmental Protection.

457 Blue Mountain Wildlife. n.d. *About Us.* Retrieved from http://www.

bluemountainwildlife.com/bmw/index.php?option=com_content&task=view&id=12&Itemid=26.

458 Commonwealth of Pennsylvania. 1980. *Schuylkill River Project Lands and Schuylkill River Scenic Designation*. Unpublished paper.

459 P.L. 1277, No. 283 of 1972.

460 P.L. 90-542, 16 USC 1271, et. Seq.

461 Pennsylvania Department of Conservation and Natural Resources. n.d. *Priority 1-A Waterways*. Retrieved from http://www.dcnr.state.pa.us/brc/rivers/scenicrivers/prioritywaterways.aspx.

462 Latham, R. 19 June 1977. "Great Outdoors: A Driving Force Behind Scenic Rivers." *Pittsburgh Press*. Retrieved from http://news.google.com/.

463 Reed, D. 12 August 1976. "River Study Is Outlined." *Reading Eagle*. Retrieved from http://news.google.com/.

464 "Greenway Unit to Stay Active." 30 November 1978. *Reading Eagle*. Retrieved from http://news.google.com/.

465 Schuylkill River Project Engineers. 1951. *op. cit.*

CPSIA information can be obtained at www.ICGtesting.com
Printed in the USA
BVOW10*2059101013

333471BV00001B/1/P

9 780985 987206